AN HONEST LIFE

In this autobiographical study Geoffrey Hooper has produced a work of compelling interest. He explores with searing honesty his struggle to affirm his integrity as a married Anglican priest who has to face the ultimate inescapable truth of his same-sex orientation. The profound internal struggle as he acknowledges that he is a gay man is paralleled by the complex ambivalence or overt hostility of the external world. Family, Church and wider society combine to create a context which demands every ounce of his emotional resilience and courage. This is a narrative illuminated at different stages by Geoffrey's understanding of priesthood, theology, psychology and therapeutic process. It also bears witness to his steadfast commitment to Christian faith in the face of difficulties which continually threaten to undermine him. The book is also beautifully written.

Professor Brian Thorne, Emeritus Professor of Counselling, University of East Anglia. Co-founder of Norwich Centre, Leading Person-centred Practitioner and Bestselling Author

Geoffrey Hooper exposes the appalling treatment his remarkable ministry has received at the hands of the Church. His work in Newham was transformative in a demanding context. At the same time his personal life was in turmoil as he struggled to liberate his own sexuality. The story is moving, a pilgrimage of faith and should be read by all those who are concerned at the way the Church manages to marginalise gay clergy.

Bishop Stephen Lowe, Retired Church of England's full-time Bishop for Urban Life and Faith

An Honest Life is the true story of a gay man of faith finding his way, his true self. Geoffrey Hooper graces the reader with a straightforward telling of his life's story without any hint of proselytizing or excusing. As a teacher of American high school students for nearly three decades, I had ample opportunity to observe teenagers begin to discover their sexuality. My experience tells me that young men are quicker to recognize their homosexuality than young women of that age. I can well imagine the comfort and validation that my gay students might have felt, had they been able to read this engaging book.

Jane Ready Hill, American High School Teacher

In 'my Father's House' could well be the title of this eloquent memoir. It is a story of faith and faithfulness. Faith in an all loving and just God, and faithfulness to Geoffrey Hooper's own father's abhorrence of cant and hypocrisy that has enabled this man to live a life of integrity and true goodness. The human authenticity and religious authenticity are one. Geoffrey's account of his lifelong painful struggle to be fully human as a gay, married, divorced priest with two children – and now grand-children – is a challenge and joy. Having finished reading the book, I felt like I had dipped my hands into the pockets of God.

Fr Bernard Lynch, Roman Catholic Priest, Psychotherapist and Bestselling Author

Woven into the tapestry of this poignant autobiography are the dreams and hopes, the struggles and wounds, that characterize many of our lives at a time when our intimate yearnings undergo profound and disturbing evolutionary growth. An inspiring and prophetic read!

Fr Diarmuid Ó Murchú MSC, Social Psychologist and Widely-read Author

An Honest Life:

Faithful and Gay

An Honest Life:

Faithful and Gay

Geoffrey Hooper

CHRISTIAN
ALTERNATIVE

Winchester, UK
Washington, USA

First published by Christian Alternative Books, 2015
Christian Alternative Books is an imprint of John Hunt Publishing Ltd.,
Laurel House, Station Approach,
Alresford, Hants, SO24 9JH, UK
office1@jhpbooks.net
www.johnhuntpublishing.com
www.christian-alternative.com

For distributor details and how to order please visit the 'Ordering' section on our website.

Text copyright: Geoffrey Hooper 2014

ISBN: 978 1 78279 921 4
Library of Congress Control Number: 2014954147

A CIP catalogue record for this book is available from the British Library.

Design: Stuart Davies

Printed in the USA by Edwards Brothers Malloy

We operate a distinctive and ethical publishing philosophy in all
areas of our business, from our global network of authors to
production and worldwide distribution.

CONTENTS

For
Rachel and Rebecca

Acknowledgement

I am grateful to friends who have helped and encouraged me during the last two years. Some have painstakingly proofread text; others who knew me well through different periods of my life have either assured me that what I have written more or less accords with what actually happened or suggested amendments; a number have proffered their personal and professional opinions that the book is publishable; and one dear friend in particular has accompanied me from beginning to end and offered honest criticism which has resulted in me abandoning more text than I have retained. I dare not mention your names for fear I leave someone out. In any case your personal journeys have long since banished egos that needed massaging. I would never have got here without you. Thank you.

Introduction

'Don't ask, don't tell' (formerly the official United States policy on gays in the military) ruled that *openly* gay personnel were barred from service whilst the *closeted* gay were encouraged. Such a policy, although invisible and unnamed, was the elephant in rooms where I grew up, and in pews I came to occupy before and after ordination. Yet during these formative years I had no idea such an elephant lay in wait for me, ready to smother my emerging alternative sexual inclinations and replace them with conforming heterosexual norms. Now, with the passage of half a century and my masks lifted, most of the Western World – including the US military – has named the elephant and set it free. My grandchildren will live in a gay-accepting world. If they or any of their descendents find they are gay their lives will be very different from mine. Today only a small – but still significant – minority of people seem to want to keep the old elephant hidden or alive at all. Sadly, this includes most of Christendom's churches where it still lurks somewhere along a continuum of attitudes ranging from the ambivalence of 'don't ask, don't tell' to a policy that advocates annihilation.

But as the veil of 'don't ask, don't tell' gradually lifts from society's attitude to varying sexualities – including sections of the Church – it seems to be descending over religious belief. Is faith in God becoming the twenty-first century elephant: the unmentionable subject? Church attendance is diminishing throughout the Western World. It is increasingly de rigueur not to admit to belief in God. Sigmund Freud's alternative menu becomes temptingly appetizing: "religious doctrines are all illusions where God is a projection brought on by the desire to revert to the state of infantile dependency."[1] *Quod erat demonstrandum*. Richard Dawkins and others proclaim: No God; nothing to believe in; no need for faith.

But people still search for answers to the big questions: the origins and purpose of life questions. Often role models like Gandhi or Mandela seem to provide more convincing answers by their examples than an avalanche of archaic and often unintelligible words floating down from pulpits. In the institutional churches, equality and justice have been empty words for the black, the gay and the female as successive consultations and debates have rolled on; humility and simplicity are bitter words for the poor and dispossessed when set against the pomp and privilege of many. Yet there are faithful disciples inside the churches too. Desmond Tutu retained Anglican faith and spoke out alongside Mandela; Liberation Theology in South America was the womb from which Pope Francis emerged; Jim Wallis, spiritual advisor to Barack Obama, has been a radical evangelical voice for peace and social justice. And countless others have stood – still stand – as beacons within the institutional churches demonstrating they have God in the centre of their *lives* and not just their religion.

An Honest Life is more than a gay coming out story, although it is that, and tries to share how it felt for someone from the inside who entered the cul-de-sac of marriage and had to face and overcome not only the hostile world around him but also his own hidden motives and unconscious drives. It is principally my own story as accurately as I can recall it, occasionally interwoven with anonymous stories of others I have loved or helped. I also try to speak openly about my personal faith: how, although I have jettisoned doctrines and practices which I find erroneous or unhelpful and moved to the margins of institutional religion, I have retained core Christian beliefs, a strong awareness of divine grace being present in my life and known at my deep centre (what a former Dean of Westminster Abbey[2] has called) "the enduring melody of God's love for me". I echo the sentiments of the Reverend Mother who said: "I believe profoundly in God: it's religion I can't be doing with."[3] Even Archbishop Michael

Ramsey confessed: "As I get older, I believe more and more about less and less!"[4]

The spiritual counsellor and writer, Lucinda Vardey, suggests that: "there are times in our lives when we long for change, when we have an insatiable need to pierce the safer boundaries of our existence to find what is beyond. We seek a sense of unity with each other, a sense of loving and being loved, of finding peace that comes when a balanced life is lived. This is a treasure found at the end of any spiritual quest: that with the right ingredients of wisdom discovered on the way, we can joyfully live in the perfection of being wholly ourselves."[5]

An Honest Life is an account of my quest to become wholly myself. I have written it hoping it might make a positive contribution to the Gay/Faith debate which never seems to fully get resolved. I hope it might be something worth sharing with:

- Those who hold that faith and active homosexuality are incompatible.
- Those who find themselves in similar circumstances to me – married with children and gay – and want to change or stay in their current situations.
- Those who are secure in their gay identity but have been put off by what they see in the Church or who simply see no place in their lives for belief in a God.
- Those who are happy with being gay themselves, and are often in committed partnerships, but choose to practise a don't ask, don't tell policy or settle for a second-class citizen status.
- Those who are heterosexual and accept those of us who are gay but have not fully grasped the implications of complete equality.
- Those who are afraid to look through psychological lenses at what lies hidden below their conscious awareness.
- Those of any sexual orientation within or outside the

Church who, baffled by the ongoing gay debate, may find this personal story helpful.

Geoffrey Hooper
October 2014
Corris
Machynlleth
Mid Wales

Chapter One

Discovery

Years Zero to Twenty-two
From the child of five to myself is but a step.
But from the new born baby to the child
of five is an appalling distance.
Leo Tolstoi

World War II broke out soon after I was born. The darkening mood of the nation echoed the black cloud that hovered over my parents. But, in the depth of their despair, William and May would have been unaware that Geoffrey Michael's astrological chart predicted a more optimistic future: despite the not inconsiderable challenges he could expect, his life would be overshadowed by a benign rainbow. Perhaps behind a frowning countenance a smiling face was hiding?

This is a chart full of purpose and promise. You have ten trines and eleven squares. The trine is the most helpful you can have and offers an opportunity for success. The square is technically a difficult aspect but it is difficult in a helpful way; it puts difficulties in a person's path thus making them make an effort to overcome difficulties. So if we have opportunity for considerable success (ten trines) and the ability to make the necessary effort to achieve that success, then good results must surely follow. In addition, most of these form a Grand Trine in which they join up together so the general effect is greatly strengthened. *From my Astrological Chart, drawn-up by David Thomas, Astrologer, in 2003.*

The difficulties began *in utero*. Because of my mother's preeclampsia, I had entered the world dramatically six weeks earlier than expected, weighing only two-and-a-half pounds – long before the days of incubators. By bringing on my premature birth our dedicated GP had defied the prediction of the gynaecologist that we could not possibly both survive. We did: my mother until she was but a wisp away from ninety. On my first Sunday my father, a man of no faith himself (as far as I knew) but probably urged on by his devout Methodist mother, arranged for an emergency baptism insisting it would be "into the proper church rather than any chapel" – an uncharacteristic initiative for him but one that subsequently had significant consequences for me.

Now, having enjoyed the arrival and development of two daughters and three grandchildren myself, I realise that to believe your little darling is unique and special is not the exclusive prerogative of a premature pre-war baby. There are sufficient photographs and family anecdotes for me to know that I was a much-loved child. My suspicion is that my mother's own insecurity prevented her from allowing me to take the necessary risks for healthy development; and my father, whose father died when he was six, had few male role models upon which he could base his own parenting skills – and also was probably jealous of my mother's transference of her affection from him to me. I soon understood that life revolved around our grocer's shop. Other children played with wooden building blocks: I was shown a box of Heinz baked beans and the shelf upon which they needed to be stacked. In less sarcastic moments, I can reflect gratefully that any social skills or sense of personal responsibility I may have developed will have their foundation in that grocer's shop: I am proud of my parents' training by personal example.

From this secure haven – particularly during those crucial first five years – I progressed out of nappies to short then long well-creased grey flannel trousers; from Wolf Cubs to Scouts, Senior Scouts and Rovers; from church chorister to altar server; from an intimate primary school where I was a confident larger fish to a prestigious boys' Grammar School where I changed into a frightened rabbit. After that my personality seemed to split: confident and outward-going at home with family and friends; taciturn and underachieving in school and similar extramural activities. To what the transmutation from bold fish to timid rabbit can be attributed I can only speculate. As an only child there were obvious social disadvantages, but my parents tried to compensate for this loss by encouraging friends and cousins to become surrogate siblings. I was bright enough to pass my eleven-plus and confident enough to sing a cheesy love song on the stage of the town's principal theatre, but between the first and second year of grammar school I plummeted from A to C stream. I used my guile to make sure I only had to endure the rough and tumble of playground, sports field or gym as little as possible. Now, seen through adult lenses, I think I can identify numerous contributory factors that might have caused my regression at the grammar school and cast their shadow over future decisions and events in my life.

It is impossible to ascribe or measure how particular events or circumstances during our formative years will fashion and shape our adult personalities. Like a mighty river, we may be able to identify humble beginnings and measure width and depth, but can only speculate about the contribution each mountain spring makes towards the relentless flow that carves its own unique course to estuary and mouth. The way in which my early fragility caused me to be protected and cosseted by family and community inevitably will have left its indelible mark. Did it leave me feeling appropriately secure and confident, or overconfident with a false sense of my personal limitations? The little boy stacking baked beans was only the first of many scenarios that contributed to me absorbing the family script – the particular shade of truth the Hoopers believed in: Work hard, serve other people and put their needs before our own. I soon learnt that if I honoured this I would be accepted into the clan and rewarded. There are countless influences from our families and cultures of origin that contribute to our progress through education; affect our choice of careers and relationships; shape our beliefs, philosophies, attitudes and lifestyles. Thus the fragile mountain spring may not grow into a mighty river, but shrivel to a rivulet or vanish from sight in a peaty bog. But I think what caused most confusion and disruption during my pubescent years was not the acceptable love of which I sang on the Pavilion Theatre stage, but the unacceptable love I was soon to discover yet dare not speak its name – that of Oscar Wilde fame.

It must be impossible for anyone born after the 1960s to make sense of my story without knowledge of some of the prevailing sociological and psychological realities during my formative years. With few exceptions secular and sacred attitudes to homosexuality were uniform. Throughout wider society homosexual people were regarded as second-class citizens, at best sick, at worst criminal; in ecclesiastical domains they were described as sinful. In a culture where deference and respect pervaded and you were brought up not to question anything you were told by your elders, the attributes of obedience and duty were mores inculcated from an early age. During my emerging adolescence nowhere was this restraining call to obedience and duty felt more keenly than in the realm of sexuality: you shouldn't or should and therefore you didn't or did – the mandatory musts, shoulds and oughts that form and drive our personal and corporate belief systems and help to shape our life scripts.

As far as I can recall between the ages of twelve and sixteen (when the word 'gay' only had its carefree, bright and showy definition) I had only been aware of homosexuality existing when first a local schoolmaster and then two scoutmasters were publicly exposed. One committed suicide; the others went to jail. I had read about these scandals in the local newspaper and joined in the school/scout tittle-tattle about them. The former was my music master. I remember my mother asking whether he had ever done anything to me. With embarrassment I answered honestly, No – without adding that I was aware that he was doing things to other boys. It was a strange twilight period for me: one of those still, breathless and expectant moments before the dawn. Although I *never* had a fantasy about the female form, homosexuality had nothing to do with me. At the same time it magnetically titillated me; attracted me like a moth to a light bulb, even though it had the potential to burn or annihilate... and all this still occurring at a level below my conscious awareness. I was aware that my father and uncles enjoyed television footage of cabaret girls dancing but knew it bored me to tears. It simply never occurred to me that I was noticing the ball boys at Wimbledon.

Inevitably a split was becoming firmly established in the grain of my personality. I talked and acted in the normative heterosexual way (the only route known in the 1950s to the Hooper Torquay grocery clan), whilst deep within myself I could only secretly think the other thing (the unspeakable one that made me tick). My naivety then was such that I was unable to recognise these inconsistent thoughts – a state known to psychologists as *cognitive dissonance*. When I was fourteen I remember first being grabbed and kissed by a girl in an airing cupboard during a party game of Sardines. The following year I walked a girl home from school and put an arm around her before she encouraged me to kiss her. At sixteen I brought a flat-chested and shorthaired girl home for tea. Between eighteen and nineteen I went out with a female work colleague to the cinema or on walks, each occasion concluding with some (for me) platonic snogging. I now realise the moment I enjoyed most was walking her home and having a cup of tea with her parents where her brother would always appear in his pyjamas. This was possibly the very first time I glimpsed a hazy awareness of my same-sex attraction. But that realisation would have been far below the level of any conscious awareness for me then.

During my sixteens and seventeens I was absorbed in moving from school into a career in a bank. In my leisure time I was immersed in scouting activities. My submerged sexual fantasies then were being fed by visions of colleagues at the bank's training college and numerous scouting activities. These were all in my mind – safe in their secret compartment – with no physical exchanges. As a child I had very occasionally dabbled in the inquisitive experiments most children get up to, and soon after puberty there had been one or two fumbling sexual exchanges with a male classmate at school which barely took the earlier experiments any further. None of these events disturbed the cultural assumption I absorbed as I was growing up: one day you will get married and have children – everyone does.

My repressed same-sex attraction did not move from head to heart until I first fell in love with another young man, but then without realising that was what had happened. My dominant fantasy was that this other boy and I would marry separate women and have children, live in adjacent semi-detached houses with connecting doors and drive similar racing green Jaguar cars with consecutive number plates. How sad and repressed can you get at seventeen? What amazing tricks your mind plays when it cannot accept an unpalatable reality? I was besotted with him; he, a year younger, hero-worshipped me. Although my feelings had a physical sexual attraction in my fantasy world, my awareness of this was so heavily repressed that it failed to ring any bells which might lead me to question my sexuality. My strongest feelings were emotional ones: he was a close friend; I loved his company; like any lovesick teenager I would happily idle away hours talking to him. I remember attending a youth conference and being allotted a double-bedded room in which we shared nothing but a half-bottle of Harveys Bristol cream sherry. On another occasion I remember us sharing a two-man tent at a scout camp and idling away a wet afternoon by inventing an innocent game where we drew with our fingers images on the other's naked back which the recipient had to identify. There was another memorable occasion walking three miles to an early morning communion service in the parish church at Widecombe in the Moor. Since then I have never heard a peal of church bells without recalling that holy walk with my first love; the melodious call to prayer wafting over distant hills. We were springing along together in step. I was in heaven. It was so innocent, so enjoyable and so normal. But, repressed deep within, there was a reservoir of sexual energy longing to unleash itself in praise of him.

My last memory during that period of our friendship was of the night my libido could hardly contain itself. We had spent a week together in the company of a mutual friend driving from John O'Groats to Land's End and back. The friend had to return early by train leaving us alone to complete the final journey. We arrived late at a farmhouse not far from Bristol to be offered a double bed as the only accommodation available. During the night every muscle in me ached to make some physical contact. A gentle game of reciprocal foot touching began, but as I tentatively advanced my approaches I realised his whole body had frozen with shock. I too froze and went back to sleep. In the morning, as he leapt out of bed to dress, I attempted to speak. I was in such agony fearing my physical action would have spoilt our deep and loving friendship that I could not speak: as I mouthed the words no audible sound would emerge. Eventually I managed to faintly mutter the one word, Sorry. "Nothing's wrong," he replied. "It's a lovely sunny morning isn't it?" Confession and absolution complete; our friendship unharmed.

I suspect this innocent first love saga – my romantic exploration from shared cream sherry to attempted sexual advances in the space of less than two years – will be a story many of my ilk and generation could probably tell. It is a sad and painful illustration of my arrested emotional and sexual development (and an omen of many more desire-pleasure-guilt-remorse-redirection cycles which were to follow). There was so little information available then to enable us to put together the dots and draw the right conclusions.

Our two paths were about to part by me being just old enough to be one of the last men in the UK to be eligible for National Service. Having half-heartedly reciprocated the sentiment when the female work colleague swore her undying love for me before I left to join the RAF, I soon wrote to explain that I had come to realise that what I felt for her was the same friendship as I felt for my male friends... and listed them all by name beginning with the one I had fallen in love with (without realising it). Still the penny did not drop. I squirm now at what I did and feel ashamed about her receiving the letter. But at last I was beginning to ask myself questions and be honest about what I felt. Unwittingly, I was taking my first tentative step on the tortuous journey towards self-understanding and self-acceptance. Somewhere in a half-conscious part of my mind I had made my first shuffle towards congruence; towards understanding my unpalatable shade of the truth; towards discovering my real self. I had allowed the two split halves of my being to at least glance at each other across the abyss and partially acknowledge each other's existence. Around this time I remember reading the novel *Giovanni's Room* by James Baldwin and being awestruck by the protagonist's account of his awakening to his gay orientation. Describing the moment of opportunity for physical commitment he exclaims: "With everything in me screaming *No!* yet the sum of me sighed *Yes*." I knew his dilemma intimately, but was not yet able to admit it – even to myself.

National service lifted me beyond the limitations of a respectable life in a provincial town and showed me a new vision which was going to change the direction and focus of my life completely. I had no intimate relationships during this time, but it should not pass without mention that I chose to celebrate my twenty-first birthday by a discreet dinner party for that elite list of male friends I annotated in the painful letter to my former girlfriend. Like the choice of same-sex extramural activities in my youth, this fact too – as far as I am aware – passed without either notice or comment by parents or other adults around me, as well as remaining below my own conscious radar.

My conscious awareness with regard to religion and spirituality seemed to follow a similar pattern. I have no recollection before the age of fifteen or sixteen of being metaphysically aware. My conscious thinking had always been practical and rational: 'spirituality' was a word that had not yet entered my vocabulary. I must have been influenced by the quasi-religious milieu in which I had spent so many of my formative years, but this never seemed to nourish me spiritually, only reinforce my altruistic bias. My paternal grandmother – the church-going Methodist – read me Old Testament stories as I sat on her lap. Up until the age of seven Sunday school teachers told me similar stories in less comfortable church pews. When followed from eight years onwards by Sunday church attendance as a chorister morning and evening, in addition to three or four intense choir practices during the week, these activities must have implanted some religious concepts. They also established important self-disciplinary patterns and a deep sense of commitment reinforcing the life script I was acquiring at home and through scouting – be good, reliable and help other people. Unsurprisingly, my favourite biblical parable became the Good Samaritan; my favourite biblical person helpful Martha. But I have no memory until my mid-teens of any deeper personal spiritual awareness.

Then there was a seismic development. When my voice broke I had to leave the church choir and my rector – with human or divine wisdom – encouraged me to become an altar server. This progression transported me from the soulless and staid environment of Sung Matins to an ethereal and meditative eight o'clock celebration of Holy Communion. It fed me at a depth I had never before experienced. Despite the disinclination of a teenager to rise early on a Sunday morning I found these sacred half-hours with only a handful of people present an oasis of peace. Here a holy spark ignited. Successive winters and summers during those formative adolescent years, on quiet, dark or sunny mornings, a quite different stirring was emerging: a still, small, silent, but tangible, movement towards the Other: unfamiliar but not frightening; compelling but not compulsive; voluntary but irresistible. As with the earlier stirring which had lurked within me unrecognised and unlabelled until it was finally named in *Giovanni's Room*, I knew again that I wanted to make the same sighing response – *Yes*! But I had no apprehension then what an explosive combination these combined ascents of *Yes* would prove to be. Very soon my saying *Yes* to such a lethal mixture of human and holy – sexual and sacred – would begin a very different war to the one which broke out shortly after my birth.

I often wonder if my father ever pondered that it could have been his insistence on me having an emergency baptism a couple of days after my birth that indirectly caused me twenty years later to make two life-changing decisions – neither of which he approved and both of which came very close to being life-shattering for me. That I might not have made either of these decisions is impossible even to contemplate now, for the consequences of my vocations to ordination and to marriage and children have indelibly shaped and defined my life.

The long trail which eventually led to ordination and marriage began with a routine medical check-up before the selection process for national service. My GP (the one who brought me into the world against all odds) asked if I wanted to do national service. If not, he said he could give me a fictitious note to disqualify me on medical grounds. To his surprise I refused the offer. At an unconscious level I seemed to realise that national service was the only way to get away – from or to what I had no idea, only some raw intuition (perhaps divine inspiration, who knows?). Despite all the military impositions and interruption of career national service brought, it seemed to offer more opportunities than restrictions. Twenty months in the rank of an RAF airman opened my eyes to life in its rawest form, making up for the rough and tumble the sheltered only child managed to avoid.

About a year into my service I was taken completely by surprise. Over a period of some six months a whole raft of unanticipated and unconnected events and encounters occurred, the sum of which gave me no option but to consider seriously whether a vocation to ordained ministry was emerging. Despite having been church chorister or altar server for ten years, nothing could have been further from my imagining – let alone my desiring – than the prospect of ordination. But the external promptings remained as I continued to bump unexpectedly into strangers or read literature with unforeseen contents which pointed towards that feared and dreaded dog collar. Eventually, in desperation and bewilderment, I wrote a convoluted letter to my home parish priest. He replied succinctly on a postcard: "I'm not a bit surprised. Remember St Paul, poor bloke, he didn't stand a chance: those whom God calls he also enables. Come and see me when next you're on leave."

The morning I went to pour out my heart was a great relief. It is difficult to convey after fifty years within or on the edge of the Church just how outrageous the thought of ordination was to me then. Banking could be seen as a progressive move up from trade but becoming a clergyman was unthinkable – academically, sociologically and financially. The whole idea was so ridiculous and fanciful to be almost laughable. It was totally alien to my familial or cultural milieu. After seeing my home rector I ran on, buoyed-up with relief and encouragement, to another clergy residence to double-check the affirming response I had just received. The scout group I had become involved in was attached to the local Congregational Church. This introduced me to their minister and the amateur dramatic society he and his wife directed. It was he to whom I ran. He offered a similar response: "Not surprised: proceed with your promptings and see what happens." It took a further four months to share my dark secret with anyone else. First my parents, where my mother left my father to advise: "You're a stupid fool; they're all a lot of hypocrites" – rather what I was anticipating and why I took four months to say anything. Second, my former bank manager employer who was expecting me to return to my old position, but simply said when I told him my news: "I'd prepared a perfect response to you telling me the RAF had offered you a commission. This is great news – let's drink to it!" Everything else seemed to unfold consequentially: formal selection as an ordination candidate of the Church of England; the offer of a place to read theology at King's College London; release from National Service; temporary employment for nine months as van driver for my father's shop.

During that nine-month gestation period, everyone – including me – was getting used to the new identity. Customers who knew me as the polite and helpful grocer's boy said, "How wonderful"; wider family members and my parents' friends expressed surprise that my father's son was going to go this way (more a reflection on my father's horse racing fanaticism than on me personally, I think); I started to learn New Testament Greek; my own friends – still in shock – formulated the usual collection of vicar jokes. Everyone seemed to use the period to adjust to the impending change in my life's direction, when they imagined I would have to stop drinking and they would have to stop swearing. None of us then had even the vaguest hint of just how different and difficult this new life was going to be.

I cannot overstate how crucial and pivotal this period of my life was: decisions made between the ages of twenty-one and twenty-four would determine almost everything that was going to happen during the following five decades. Looking through my parents' lenses, for me to have taken the leap from a safe and potentially prosperous future career into totally unknown and alien ecclesiastical territory was incomprehensible: Hoopers did not do that sort of thing. Through my own lenses it was different. However unfamiliar the alluring territory was I had *experienced* those vocational pulls first hand: to me they were real and tangible. In addition, although I was not aware of it at the time, socially I was on an upwardly mobile track. I was on the way out of the world of trade, where I never knew whether I was working or middle class, into the comfortable arms of the tier above – where grammar school boys belonged and I felt more at home.

Since my unannounced visit to share my vocational promptings with the congregational minister I had come to know him and his wife a little more through their dramatic society, but been unaware that they had a daughter. They asked if I could kindly accompany her to a local ecumenical meeting whilst they were on holiday. I agreed, little realising that this innocent act of neighbourly helpfulness would soon turn into a relationship with the same fate as the maiden voyage of the Titanic.

The next significant stage in my vocational journey came when I set forth from Torquay in bright sunshine on a crisp autumn morning in 1961: three keen young men in a Morris Minor coupé eager to take their places as freshers at university – the driver bound for Bristol; front passenger (my first love) bound for Southampton; and me in the back seat (dressed in blazer proudly with London University tie, duffle coat and trilby) bound for the metropolis. I could have been a twelve year old setting out for boarding school for the first time: such was my innocence and naiveté.

My pre-college gestation period had included (what would

have been called in those days) a gentle courtship with the
minister's daughter – not a lot different from the experience with
the former bank colleague, except for greater involvement with
her parents. Her mother, particularly, was aware of the social gulf
between the two families and worked tactfully to knit bonds
between the mothers. With the wisdom of hindsight, I know what
I felt towards the daughter was the fondness of friends who share
some interests, for us mainly around Anglican matters. My
feelings were nothing like those I had for my first love. When she
read me love poetry I neither associated it with feelings I had for
him (because those were still repressed), nor could I associate it
with feelings I had for her (because I simply did not have them).
Nevertheless, I am ashamed to say that I assented to her
suggestion that these were reciprocal feelings for us both. This
sounds incredibly callous and duplicitous now, but then I was
either blind to the emotional realities in which I was becoming
enmeshed or too petrified to acknowledge them.

Although my true inner feelings for my girlfriend had limited
depth, before that autumn day when my friends and I set sail for
London, we had a mutual swearing of undying love – not
dissimilar to the time I left the former bank colleague for national
service. For my girlfriend it will have been very different, for she
had fallen deeply in love. Letters were exchanged between us
with increasing frequency during term time when I was at King's,
and my deepening entanglement with her and her family
continued during the vacations. It felt to me as though I was
somewhere along the continuum from 'being absorbed' to 'being
taken over', and as though I had little control over what was
happening. Recalling this half a century later, it sounds pathetic.
But as far as I can honestly reflect, that is how it was as I was
experiencing it then. I can now see how much damage my
emotional ignorance – or fear of rejection – must have caused.
Without consciously realising it, I led her along; misled not only
her and both our families but myself too. It was not clinical self-

deception (that came later), for I simply had no conscious concept or understanding of who or what I was. Now I can understand how it was a continuation of my self-denial of those forbidden and unimaginable feelings about which I dared not even think, let alone ask myself questions.

There was another motive for my developing relationship of which I was also in denial. This is best conveyed through part of a case study for a former counselling client of mine, a young man the same age as I was then:

He has been in successive relationships with three or four girlfriends since he was sixteen. They have all had supportive middle class families who have welcomed him as part of their family. His own background has been fraught from birth onwards: father deserted two or three times during his first ten years – now vanished; a number of disastrous stepfathers; mother who's sustained him closely, but lived in poverty amidst domestic violence. From the age of twelve, through a generous scholarship, he went to a prestigious public boarding school where he showed great academic promise but never finally achieved. He is now able to reflect back and see the tension he had to bear by being part of a privileged school life (particularly when staying with friends in vacations), and the instability and poverty of his own home life. He can see how he has chosen a succession of unsuitable girlfriends in order to be part of their families and thereby experience something he never had, but always longed for.

Although my situation was not nearly as extreme as his, I too adored being part of the minister's family: joining their holidays in a remote country cottage; walking together over Devonshire moorland; reading novels aloud by a log fire; enjoying cultured conversation during evening meals. Through their accepting, patient tutoring I was becoming middle class. I loved it, became fond of them, and will always be grateful for that gift.

Formulated during the latter years of the nineteenth century, Sigmund Freud's concepts of the unconscious and of the levels of consciousness are considered to be among his greatest contributions to understanding behaviour and problems of personality. His hypotheses, along with insights from twentieth century systemic theory about the effect family and cultural influences have on personal development, have helped my understanding enormously. I now see why it took me so long and cost me so much emotionally to come to terms with such a fundamental aspect of my human constitution. I see how, at those formative stages of my life, living under the umbrella of the social mores that prevailed, I had little choice but to deny or distort reality in order to protect myself (and others close to me) from the horrific implications of my same-sex attraction. My particular shade of truth – the only shade I was able to have for my human desiring – was more than forbidden fruit: for me it was an unthinkable reality. A significant strand of the *life script* I was acquiring from my familial and cultural milieu (learnt opinions, habits, attitudes and behaviour) was the fear of confrontation: 'circumnavigate a difficult situation in any possible way you can rather than challenge it head on and become unpopular'. This automatic internal response will have undoubtedly contributed to the way I was unable to face the essential reality of my sexuality and will have transmuted into a defence mechanism. Within psychodynamic and psychoanalytical understanding, various *defences* (in my case over issues regarding sexuality – denial, displacement, projection, splitting and repression) gradually crept in and became permanent fixtures in the way I related to the outer world. I see how easy it was for me gradually to develop a cycle of desire-pleasure-guilt-remorse-redirection whenever Eros raised its dreaded head.

Seen through the lenses of another twentieth century

psychotherapeutic model – a Person-centred understanding – I was gradually moving from my actual self (the present reality of my life) towards my true self (my innate being): what Carl Rogers, the American psychologist and therapist, referred to as *The Actualizing Tendency*. Although I had been hindered by the external restraints and expectations of others I was moving in the direction of my personal truth – what Rogers believes is for everyone an active drive or motivating force from birth, the purpose of which is to enable us to achieve wholeness. Rogers saw this as a deeply instinctive – primal – movement towards the light, from incongruence to congruence.

Although it would increasingly prove to be a difficult and painful road for me to embark upon, once the Light had been glimpsed it was the only route I could take: all the defences I had put in place to protect myself from painful realities had to be confronted and redeemed – whatever the cost.

Chapter Two

Denial

Years Twenty-three to Thirty-one
I went to the Garden of Love,
And saw what I never had seen;
A chapel was built in the midst,
Where I used to play on the green.
And the gates of the chapel were shut,
And 'thou shalt not' writ over the door;
So I turn'd to the Garden of Love
That so many sweet flowers bore;
And I saw it was filled with graves,
And tomb-stones where flowers should be;
And Priests in black gowns were walking their rounds,
And binding with briars my joys and desires.
William Blake

During my first term at King's, I was blown away by the experience of being in London. It was another world. I strutted around The Strand in my pristine gown, attended lectures assiduously and wallowed in being waited upon at table at the Westminster theological hostel. I sampled churches and more alluring London venues avidly – including afternoon tea at the Savoy. But, above all, I was intrigued by and absorbed in the rich blend of personalities and backgrounds which the undergraduates of King's comprised. During minor excursions visiting cousins south of the river during the 1950s, I vowed I could never live in London. Now, after three months, I was in love with it. Was this what I had intuitively sensed when the GP offered me the fictitious note that would have locked me into the West Country forever? This was freedom. I was flying. I seldom gave a thought about Torquay in between letters arriving or vacations beginning.

At the end of my first year, aware that the summer vacation ahead would last for three long months, I can see now that I acted out my internal struggle over repressed sexual identity by pre-empting the pressure that I felt was mounting for me to be continually with my girlfriend for the whole of that period. Still at only about a quarter-conscious level of understanding my true motive (to avoid the inevitable growing intimacy expected by her), I accepted an invitation to spend a few weeks of the vacation living with the family of an Old Testament professor in Oxford and working as a chauffeur-cum-au pair to three small children. It was true that "help with biblical studies and experience of pastoral ministry" was on offer as remuneration, but the arrangement was totally voluntary. I told everyone it was a mandatory requirement of my training. This was a lie. Psychologists might more kindly – and accurately – describe it as pathological behaviour and an example of the power of self-deception, expressing something of the fear I was experiencing about those unspeakable internal thoughts and temptations. But my true self knew what I was doing and why I was doing it, even if my actual self was unable yet to express congruence through my actions.

King's then would have been considered to be a liberal-to-catholic theological college at the radical cutting edge academically, spiritually and pastorally. Discreetly, there existed within the body of theological students (some 180 men) one or two ad hoc clusters of four or five, shall we say, men who knew they were probably not going to get married. Most theological colleges would not have any such cliques, overtly; one or two seemed to be comprised of little else. This whole phenomenon was an eye-opener for me. Innocently, I had come only to learn how to be a vicar. But my antennae could not resist absorbing like blotting paper every camp gesture or sentence. Innuendos abounded. I hovered on the edge of the cohorts, neither in nor out. At any conscious level I was unaware I was there, or that there was a 'there' to be. During the first term of my second year I tagged along with one of these groups to see the newly released film *Victim*. Initially banned in the USA, it became highly controversial in the UK. Dirk Bogarde plays the part of a successful married barrister involved in a romantic, but asexual, relationship with a young man who was being blackmailed – who eventually hanged himself. The film addresses the issues facing a professional married man wrestling with his sexuality. It had greater significance for me than *Giovanni's Room*, not only because of its visual impact, but because the protagonist was a married man. Perhaps it should have acted as a wake-up call? Instead I only felt it as the tremor of an earthquake might be felt by a frightened and mystified primitive community: it disturbed my comfortable heterosexual facade to the bones, but left me only with more bewilderment and still no personal enlightenment.

The therapeutic world knows that enlightenment (the moment when we see through our protective defences even if we choose not to remove our masks) seldom happens as an instantaneous event: no Damascus Road flash, only seeing truth and acting upon it gradually. My early glimpses of such threatening awareness were so frightening that it was as though I slammed shut the trapdoor that protected my pre- or sub-conscious awareness from such menacing material which, because it was so terrifying, had long been banished to dark and hidden vaults of unconsciousness for fear of the pain it would inflict on me if it escaped anywhere near my conscious awareness. Me – one of those? No. No. No. Never!

I was known to have a girlfriend at home, so from the perspective of the ad hoc gay cohorts I was not one of them. Just as species in the wild reject those who are different from their own kind, I thought I was disregarded by the cohorts. But I was soon to learn that some of them had suspected me long before I understood myself. A group of us was returning from East London after a visit to the boys' boxing club which King's sponsored. I was sitting on the back seat of a Morris Mini alongside the President of the Theological Faculty, a third year student. Silently, in the darkness, as we passed Cleopatra's Needle on the Embankment, he clasped my hand. Warning lights from *Giovanni's Room* and *Victim* flashed before my eyes: "With everything in me shrieking *No!* yet the sum of me sighed *Yes.*" And the *Yes* won – quickly followed, not by disgust or remorse, but by total shock and more confusion. Simultaneously I was in heaven and in hell.

Because I was a student preparing for ordination under obedience to my superiors, I went straight to the sub-warden of the college (a trusted priest who was my personal director and confessor) and poured out my confused heart with total honesty. "It's quite natural to feel like that now. When you're married the feelings will go away," was his pastoral reply. With echoes from the book and the film still resounding somewhere between my unconscious and conscious awareness, I knew at a gut level this was not true. Within the week I went to the Dean of King's and cried for his help. Back came the exact same reply. They must be right. I believed them. And down came the quarter-open trapdoor to my conscious awareness: slam! Within that moment, any actualizing tendency seemed to go into reverse gear and I moved backwards along the track from congruence to incongruence, away from my true self. Now I did not even have to think of asking myself those difficult questions: my mentors' comfortable answers had removed that requirement. I returned to Torquay for the vacation as though nothing had happened – book and film forgotten. My denial was now reinforced through those responsible for my preparation for ordination: it felt as though an 'imprimatur' had been issued by them. In future, any tempting thoughts that came into my head were benign because I was assured they would cease when I became married. Had I

been given what today would be considered responsible professional therapeutic intervention, how different the ensuing years
might have been?

In the early 1960s society still expected responsible heterosexual
couples – particularly ordination candidates – who were dating
regularly to demonstrate their intentions on the third finger of
the woman's left hand. In the summer vacation of my second
year, during the Congregational minister's annual family holiday
on Dartmoor, it was becoming embarrassing for me. I knew what
was expected of me, but my confused and deeply hidden secret
impeded my progress when I attempted to take the plunge.
Towards the end of the holiday there were fairly overt hints being
lovingly given by the others. I decided I could prevaricate no
longer and resolved to say something, but found the words
simply would not come out of my mouth – ironic echoes of
waking up with the first love. Eventually, prompted by my
fiancée-in-waiting, we were able to return from a walk with news
that we would like to become engaged – permission from father-
in-law and church authorities, respectively, being expected and
required.

But during the night in between the first failed and second
successful attempt at a proposal, I had the most horrendous
struggle. Painful promptings sprang from gut and heart – but not
yet the head – from the unconscious box into which I had
banished them. The ravages of hell had broken out. It was as
though I was wrestling in dark hidden depths of an ocean where
mythical sea monsters lurked. I lay awake much of the night
praying in my single bedroom for divine intervention. Seen
through both psychological and theological lenses, either a red
warning light was blinding me and still I could not find the
courage to heed it, or a green one was reassuringly coaxing me
forward. I chose to believe it was the latter. Was I colluding with
the *don't ask, don't tell* culture that surrounded me in church

circles? Was my desire to be accepted into the middle class strata so strong that I deluded myself I was really heterosexual and therefore there were no awkward questions to ask? Had hetero-sexism imbedded itself so deeply that I was unable to face my truth?

It is impossible to assess with any accuracy what quantitative contribution my desire to comply with the heterosexual expectations around me made – or just my desire to join the minister's family. I suspect both contributed to my prevailing construct. I know years later in personal therapy, after marital disaster had struck, I described how I felt during those years of courtship:

> It was as though I was inside a well-greased metal funnel, with a blindfold over my eyes, panicking and trying to climb up towards the lip in order to reach my true sexual orien-tation, but continually sliding back down towards the spout where my heterosexual destiny lay. The greased funnel, with its downward gravity pull, represented the community around my fiancée and me: "Local well-respected grocer's son, now a theological student and future vicar, with the local well-respected congregational minister's daughter – obviously a marriage made in heaven," acclaimed customers and parishioners alike. To me, the pull of gravity seemed unassailable and I felt compelled (against the deeper warnings of my true self wanting to climb up and get out) to go with that downward pull towards the feared heterosexual spout.

After the summer vacation I returned to London to begin my final academic year at King's by announcing my engagement. Although the theological faculty was considered to be at the radical cutting edge compared with other theological colleges in the 1960s, I did not then have the psychological balance or personal maturity to absorb and benefit from the rich academic and spiritual gifts on offer. I was too preoccupied with unresolved internal struggles: my place within the social structure and my confused sexuality. Even from their submerged unconscious depths these concerns were still eating away in the foreground of my priorities: like an impatient toddler they were demanding instant attention and satisfaction. The absent formal ingredient during our time of preparation for ordination seemed to be personal psychological insight. King's included some input in this field (much more than most theological colleges) but it was fed only at a theoretical level and failed to penetrate below the mind to gut and heart. I needed a lifeline – grappling hook possibly – to help me penetrate deeper. Spiritually self-blind-folded, my ego was fed by being elected president of the theological faculty. I spread my wings with students from other faculties, becoming infatuated with a physicist – benignly, I still thought, because my mentors had assured me this feeling would soon go away.

Alas, I enjoyed the new social stimulation so much that I forgot that in a few months I had some important final examinations to sit. To my horror, when the results came I found I had failed. Disaster had struck. To be president of the faculty and fail your finals was unheard of. The outcome was that I could not continue on with my peers to the fourth year college, but had to spend a year out to retake two papers. I was totally humiliated and distraught. The Psalmist's words resounded: *Thou shalt bruise them with a rod of iron: and break them in pieces like a potter's vessel.* Within the frameworks of both vocational faith and personal development it was probably the best thing that could have happened to me: it burst my inflated ego and brought me down to earth. I returned to Devon with my head hung low. A decision was made to marry in the autumn, live in an unoccupied curate's house and find work locally whilst I retook the two papers before proceeding to the last year's theological training with my wife. Any pretentions about social positioning seemed cured after my fall from grace: I was secure in my vocation and my professional status but now, hopefully, cloaked in much needed humbleness.

Other things had not changed. I obtained temporary work at a male dominated Outward Bound school. The physicist whom I had fallen for became the best man at our wedding – joining the first love who was an usher. Three months after the wedding I realised that the same-sex attractions had not fallen away, as I had been promised they would: they were worse. I was totally infatuated with the physicist, even though he lived two hundred miles away and was shortly getting married himself. I remember, secretly and alone one day at the Outward Bound school, taking a crate of empty milk bottles and smashing them one by one against a brick wall in anger and frustration, totally aware of why I was taking this destructive action. A year later whilst at the fourth year college, just after my wife's planned pregnancy was known, during the three-hour midday devotions on Good Friday, I silently screamed my wrath at God for letting me down: I was still finding my strong attractions to men around me were impossible to suppress. I was now trapped: married, about to become a father and ordained, yet still obsessed by these secret longings. Nevertheless I resolved to be a loyal priest, faithful husband and loving father: I would set my hands to the plough without turning back, and keep these other thoughts at bay.

Eighteen months earlier my bride and I had glided up the central aisle of her father's church believing we were dancing into the sunset. On the surface, we entered a fairy tale world on the day of our ceremony – as all newlyweds do. The whole world loves a wedding, not least my parents' local customers and my parents-in-law's parishioners. Everyone seemed to bask in the sunshine and wish us well. Some perhaps projected on to us their own dashed hopes and expectations, but no one would have realised the hidden fear which my smiling face camouflaged as I antici-pated activities that would have to be undertaken during the honeymoon. There was excitement in setting-up the new home and believing we were now fully adult and independent. It is difficult to convey to those who have not been through the matrimonial experience just how powerful and seductive it is. For the day, and for sometime after it, you *are* a prince and princess: the community welcomes you into their most popular club and showers you with presents. At least, that is how it felt to me in 1964... on the surface.

Underneath, it was very different. I did not experience the relief of being a couple alone or the joy of intimacy, because I could not. I could see how much pleasure it brought my wife and was glad for her. But the feelings were simply not there for me. I feared both the couple solitude and the intimacy. For me it was so different. It was enjoyable to feel properly adult and independent, but this was fundamentally different from experiencing personal ecstasy. I only fully realised what I felt then *was different in kind* to the feelings my wife enjoyed when years later I experienced that ecstasy and joy with a same-sex partner: then I moved from black and white into technicolour.

In his groundbreaking book, *Virtually Normal*, Andrew Sullivan expresses my feelings and experiences perfectly as he describes his escape from England to America:

(It was) another country where I could come home. I remember my first kiss with another man, the first embrace, the first love affair. Many metaphors have been used to describe this delayed homecoming – I was twenty-three – but to me, it was like being in a black and white movie that suddenly converted to colour. The richness of the experience seemed possible for the first time; the abstractions of dogma, of morality, of society, dissolved into sheer, mysterious pleasure of being human.[6]

Even now I am so sorry I could not bring this mutuality to our marital relationship. I can see now how throughout the thirteen years of our marriage I unconsciously compensated for the lack of depth of commitment I was able to allow in our relationship by practical acts of kindness and support – housework, childcare, generous material gifts. This is not the same as a couple who develop their mutual interdependent entwining during those early days of their union. But, because neither of us had passed the way of coupledom before, I suspect both of us were not fully aware of what was missing. Personal intimacy was an essential ingredient I was incapable of either offering or receiving: I could only offer and receive in the way I was capable of doing as a gay man in a straight man's clothing. This is not the place to discuss these details, but suffice it to say bedroom activity had more of a quantitative than qualitative contribution: there was an expectation to be met and duty to be done but, sadly, there could be no magical and transformational experience for me.

For the next six or seven years I tried to keep the promise I had made on that Good Friday a few weeks before my ordination: to commit myself to being a faithful husband, loving father and loyal priest. But it was a battleground for me continually having to ward off temptation. After the college year together, for just under four years we ministered in Chesterfield as curate and wife: a challenging and stressful period with limited practical, emotional and financial support after the birth of our first daughter, and with major professional challenges in the parish. It was not easy for either of us. My new wife had to adjust to the contrast of middle class protection in a Free Church manse to life in a terraced house amidst a mining community and a new husband whose work demanded his absence most evenings and all weekends. The parish had had decades of history with single clergy, on whom parishioners showered the usual Anglo-Catholic 'Father' sycophantic adoration. They seemed hardly to notice a struggling wife who, after an extremely stressful birth, was left with what would now be diagnosed as postnatal depression causing mother/child attachment difficulties. My memory is that the first eighteen months of our much welcomed daughter's life were overshadowed by the combined parish and domestic demands: a gallon being poured into a pint pot from so many directions, internally and externally.

Within psychoanalytical theory, hard work and family duty would be seen to have contained at least an element of *sublimation* for the dimension that was missing in my married life. The shadow that had always been there never left my fantasy life. My expectation that these things would be removed through marriage was not helped by finding that two fellow curates – also both married – were living in similar circumstances. Perhaps everyone had these shadows? But even at that early stage of my limited psychological understanding, I should have known I was not focusing on any issue of bisexuality: I was someone who should have not been in a heterosexual marriage. Two years into my curacy I mentioned my secret invasive thoughts to my new bishop during a routine annual appraisal. They were still causing me agony: I just did not know what to do. History repeated itself: "I'm sure you'll find it lessens as you grow into your marriage. I will pray for you." Shortly after this Episcopal advice was proffered an incident occurred – at another man's instigation – which moved me a notch further towards congruence. It poured petrol on to my smouldering suppressed flame and, although giving me a fleeting taste of heaven, took me deeper into hell. Without realising it at the time, it brought me nearer to accepting the personal truth which would eventually be my salvation.

This Achilles heel at the core of my being (still smothered in the mists of semi-conscious suppression for me and innocent unawareness for my wife) must have exacerbated the strain we were both experiencing from the external demands we were trying to cope with. Any repression or suppression of painful material can be a ripe seedbed for psychosomatic illnesses. It undoubtedly will have contributed to my wife's depression, and on one significant occasion manifested itself in me. I had developed a mysterious infection which produced extreme lethargy and a constant fever for some weeks. I was referred to two different specialists for suspected glandular fever and suspected deep-rooted tonsil infection. Both drew blanks. After a month or two off work I gradually recovered. It was only some twenty years later that my mother out of the blue proclaimed: "I knew at the time you were having a nervous breakdown." Mothers usually do know! Only then did I silently remember that my father-in-law had privately asked me if there was anything worrying me. He was the only person who made any psychosomatic connection, but I do not think he would have had any inkling of my internal struggles at that time. I certainly was a long way from making any conscious connection myself, although would have been perfectly aware cognitively that this was the way our emotions and bodies interconnect. It was far too close for comfort for me to apply theory to personal reality. Now it is my daily bread to suggest such connections for others within a professional therapeutic setting: in 1968 I saw only through that particular glass very darkly.

My first working day after ordination in Derby Cathedral had offered a cameo of an aspect of parish ministry that I found increasingly difficult to tolerate. Bright-eyed with smart new dog collar, my car having failed to start, I ran two miles to the parish church for Morning Prayer with my colleagues at 7.30am. They arrived twenty minutes late, with neither apology nor welcome. The staff meeting that followed in the vicar's study revealed bitter rifts between verger, organist and clergy. I was informed that my job in the afternoon was to carry the banner in the front of a Diocesan Mothers' Union procession into church. Afterwards I was to attend the area's Anglican Clergy gathering. There I found my new fellow clergy, when not ripping each other apart, seemed only to share gossip about those who were absent. Was *this* my vocation? What had I joined? I began a painful professional journey discovering the irrelevance of much that the institutional church occupies itself with, and how readily many clergy can evade spiritual exploration by displacing energy on to irrelevant and comforting substitutes. Had the Church let me down just as it had over those other thoughts which had not gone away? I was quickly realising there were more questions to ask than just those about sexuality.

My curacy was a time when, like all professional fledglings, I wanted to make my mark and impress. Just as there is a field marshal's baton in every soldier's kitbag, curates believe they have the perfect legs for gaiters! Although my vicar and fellow curates brought a radical theological and social perspective into a traditional and old-fashioned Anglo-Catholic parish, they seemed to offer a detached academic and rather cynical contribution which lacked any common touch or transcendental dimension to a down to earth and spiritually thirsty local community. It felt as though an enormous burden had landed on my fragile shoulders as people turned towards me for pastoral support. I would have been considered by my clerical colleagues as lightweight intellectually, and within the team became marginalized by my vicar and first senior curate. Pastorally, I jumped into the empty vacuum, assiduously visiting and making my mark with the young of the parish – all do and go with little time for reflection and being.

My vicar's and two fellow-curates' shortcomings, plus the expectations and projections of dependent parishioners, plus my wife's depression and daughter's infant dependency, all took their toll. At the end of my first year I remember being required to write an essay for the bishop entitled *Vision, Expectation and Reality*. I retrieved my first theoretical draft before it dropped through the mouth of the post box, tore it up and rewrote a factual account of what disappointing hell it all was. The bishop's chaplain phoned first thing next morning to call me in later that day. I pleaded with the bishop, "I simply can't fit it all into a twenty-four hour day and seven day week." The only solace he could offer was how he and his wife – no children – would sit up in bed in the morning with a cup of tea and their diaries to plan the day: it all worked out wonderfully. We lived in different worlds. Like everyone else, I had to learn the hard way.

Coming up to the four-year point in my curacy, the family was still under considerable strain all round. I floated the possibility that we consider a short-term chaplaincy in the RAF. My wife was delighted. At a pragmatic level, I think we both instinctively knew that this would be more congenial and fulfilling. As long as I eclipsed my pacifist concerns about being part of a fighting machine and replaced them with the pastoral contribution I could make it was a viable escape route. I did not allow thoughts about it being a dominantly male environment to enter my conscious awareness at any level which might prevent me from completing the application form, although I know this awareness lay very close to the trapdoor under which such secrets were stored.

The move was deemed to be a great success. My wife and daughter took to it like a duck and duckling to water. They saw more of me in the evenings and at weekends, and all of us enjoyed the company of kindred spirits in the officers' married quarters and mess. I was in paradise. I was deemed to be "great with the men" – a phrase I shall never forget coming from the lips of my first commanding officer. I was promoted three months early to the rank of Squadron Leader and asked to be chaplain at a new navigation school. By this time planned daughter number two was on the way. We were all round pegs in a perfectly fitting round hole. The new world we were in seemed to be our oyster. On the surface, my two vocations – to ordination and to marriage and children – were flourishing. But underneath, nothing had changed for me. *Don't ask, don't tell* awkward questions, both ones about sexuality and ones about faith, do not evaporate. They either have to be faced or you have to be prepared to suffer the consequences of their repression or, in my case by then, 'suppression' (for by this time I was beginning to consciously 'push down' my growing awareness of both my true sexuality and my scepticism about many Church doctrines and practices).

Chapter Three

Acceptance

Years Thirty-two to Thirty-four
Patience, which allows people to change and
situations to evolve and work themselves out;
which knows that time eventually must pass and
that successive crises have been lived through before,
both globally and personally;
and a sense of the ridiculous which can keep things
in proportion and help us to apply in daily life the
knowledge that God matters most to us all: these necessary
virtues enable us to be open to surprises and ready for risks.
Mother Jane SLG

I can probably track the embryonic turning point where I moved from the mindset of *'not asking to asking and not telling to telling'* to a Friday morning when I was called into the station commander's office to be informed that I was being posted for nine months to an unaccompanied (without family) chaplaincy on an island in the Persian Gulf. We had always known such a tour of duty would come along one day: all chaplains had to have their turn. I rode my bicycle home for lunch to break this difficult news knowing how it would affect my family and make it genuinely difficult for me to leave them. But simultaneously I also knew – now at hardly a suppressed level of conscious awareness – that my family would be replaced by an all male community.

I threw myself into the new work enjoying every minute. It was a unique opportunity for a chaplain: everyone was in the same boat, separated from their families, with a lot of time on their hands. There would be plenty of opportunity for pastoral care and outreach. I tried to make the chaplaincy complex a comfortable neutral oasis, where everyone was welcome – of all faiths and none – and treated as equals. Open and frank discussion of relevant issues about faith and social concern was encouraged. It was the only public space on the island which did not sell alcohol and where you did not have to salute the rank above you. My nine months became some of the most pastorally productive and rewarding during my years of ministry.

It being long before the advent of modern technology, communication with my family at home was limited to letters, one short telephone call at Christmas, plus a week's break with my wife in Cyprus halfway through the tour. For my five year old daughter, who had bonded closely with me before I left, my absence was a great wrench: even the regular exchange of reel-to-reel tapes could not begin to compensate for normal daily contact. My younger daughter, just two years when I returned, memorably asked who it was in Mummy's bed. "Daddy, of course," replied her sister. Younger daughter ran to her room and returned with her bedside photograph of me exclaiming: "This is Daddy." She and I had to start again from scratch with our relationship. In the services everyone is in the same boat and to a degree this might dilute the long-term effect familial separations have, but inevitably there will always be scars. In our role as parents, my wife and I did everything we could to lessen the burden of separation for the children. As individuals, the consequences for me were very different from those of my wife. The never-to-be-spoken-of secret that I had submerged for so long was quickly rising from unconscious to conscious domains of my awareness – the presence of twelve hundred men not being insignificant. But still I wanted to try to hold to my resolve to be a loyal priest, faithful husband and loving father – succeeding, save for an exchange with a father of three who shared the same hidden secret. For my wife, the prospect of a long separation had been daunting. Rather than stay at our air force base in the company of other grass widows and their children she decided to return to live with her parents, who were able to offer both emotional and practical support.

During my long period of absence she became depressed – information I was first given in a letter from my father-in-law. Her depression became apparent to me when we met for our mid-tour holiday in Cyprus, but was manifestly clear when I returned after nine months away. I was desperate to be reunited with the children and first enjoyed a sunny three-week holiday on our beloved Dartmoor before my next posting in the UK, during the first few months of which my wife's depression deepened. We struggled to cope with day to day living – demands of a new job, involvement in the community, care of a six and two year old – and tried to discover the root of her depression. Revelations about her life whilst I was overseas caused us to turn for help to *Relate* (then the National Marriage Guidance Council), first with my wife attending alone. Soon it was suggested I should attend too, which initially I could see little point in doing. Over a two or three-month period of joint counselling we seemed to be getting nowhere until an unexpected event changed the direction of our marriage and tested my faith to its limits. For me that event was simultaneously catastrophic and liberating. After it I knew my place too was in the therapist's chair.

The transformative event was the annual chaplains' conference. There I was introduced to another chaplain I had previously never met. Sexual electricity struck immediately, dangerously and gloriously. I wrestled with my dilemma for some weeks, exchanging letters with the colleague who had an overseas posting. Soon I realised this was more than a passing phase which could be shrugged off – the response to temptations I had chosen to maintain during the previous ten years of my marriage. I approached my counsellor with the information, which was the first time I had spoken about these things with anyone other than the two college staff, my first bishop and my friend during the unaccompanied tour. I acknowledged my long identified but deeply hidden feelings, and said I felt in view of what had happened at the clergy conference I needed to share this information openly with my wife. Responding appropriately in his therapeutic role, he reflected back the conclusion I had reached and left me to return home and spill the beans.

After the children went to bed I invited my wife to sit down and nervously, as sensitively as I could, explained how I had met this person and how I was attracted to him. Although for me it was a very difficult thing to do, simultaneously it was an enormous relief: no more deception; one more shuffle towards integrity and truth. But for my wife, understandably, it was excruciatingly painful. She often reflected subsequently that had my news been about someone of the opposite sex then it would have been easier; she could compete with another woman. That it was a man to whom I was attracted only left her with self-persecutory thoughts about her personal inadequacy. She was totally devastated and announced she could not stay under the same roof with me, spent the night at a friend's house and in the morning asked me to drive her to her parents, a hundred and seventy miles away.

Without notice, we arrived on the steps of the manse at six o'clock with suitcases and two children: "We need to talk after the children are in bed." The four of us sat in my father-in-law's study until midnight. We poured out our stories – for they knew nothing of our marital complications – and repeated the same procedure the following day. On the third day I had to return to my base, and my wife and children stayed with her parents. This began a period of six months' informal separation.

In the early 1970s, although greater understanding about homosexuality was emerging, there was still a long way to go within society at large – and certainly the institutional churches and armed forces – before equality could be afforded: apart from selected professions and locations, it was still a hostile world in which to be openly gay. Without giving any details, I explained to my employers that we were having marital problems and received sympathetic understanding and encouragement to try and work things through. My wife and parents-in-law insisted I inform my parents of the situation as they would be writing to them. Although I had taken the important first step of being honest with my wife and experienced the relief of not having to be duplicitous anymore, I was only just beginning to understand the inevitable consequences of my revelation: it became like a set of dominoes falling one after the other. I faced my parents, who were innocently bewildered. They were not surprised about the marital struggle, but ill equipped to deal with the other information which they simply could not talk about: they could only listen to what I had to say about my confusion. I returned to the marriage counsellor and received some support as I digested the rapidly unfurling consequences of my original revelation. I travelled fortnightly the 340 mile round trip to keep contact with the children and got on with my job without anyone realising the confusion that was raging inside their padre. I ate more often in the mess; found myself gradually being excluded from officers' social events; allowed my own married quarter to gather dust. I too was beginning to get depressed. It was agonizing for me to be separated from my children. All the adults involved were bruised and in shock. We were splashing around in unfamiliar waters with few buoyancy aids to keep us afloat. At that stage it was probably not so difficult for the children. They had recently spent nine months with Granny and Grandad when I was overseas so at first a further period of separation must have seemed just an extension of that time. They were protected from the adult whirlwind and told that Daddy's work took him away again. But as time extended to six months the absence of their father, their loss of friends and change of school will have inevitably brought its infant strain. They must also have intuited that things were far from normal: children – like animals – always do.

Then came Black Friday. As I arrived routinely in my chaplain's office at eight-thirty the phone was ringing. The Station Commander (who with his wife had become good friends) informed me that an officer from the Special Investigation Branch was walking over to my office to see me. Nothing else. I had perhaps eight or nine minutes to slip into the adjacent church and utter some silent prayers, not on my knees but walking around the aisles in an agitated state. I knew the Special Branch procedures well: if there was a matter to be investigated, initially an officer of equal rank would undertake the interview. I had no idea what I was going to be interviewed about but knew it was not going be an enquiry to the padre about someone else, as often it had been in the past. In my gut I knew it would be me that would be in the dock, and had a pretty shrewd idea what the focus of the subject matter might be. But how? Everything had been so discreet. My heart pounded; my mouth went dry; my stomach felt as though it was going to implode.

With hardly any introduction the officer started: "Padre, I have to inform you that simultaneously Padre *xyz* is being interviewed by a colleague at RAF station *abc*." He continued his interrogation as any policeman might: "On the evening of Thursday 18 October all telephone calls out of RAF stations in Germany were being recorded – a routine procedure which occurs every month. The content of the call made to your married quarter was found to be, umm… unusual…" He asked me to explain what the other chaplain was inferring by what he said.

So now I knew what had happened. I answered as honestly as I could, explaining that the other chaplain and I had met at a conference and acknowledged our mutual attraction; that I had informed my wife and we were attending marriage guidance counselling; that she and the children were with her parents; that I had written to the other chaplain saying that I had given this information to my wife and she had fled to her parents; that when he received my letter he had made this telephone call stating (as they would have heard from the tape recording) that my marriage was sacrosanct and we must never meet again. I realised then that the authorities must have not known what to make of the call because it was so brief and coded. The main thing the investigating officer wanted to know was whether there had been any "physical involvement". I replied in the negative, fully knowing that if I had admitted any I would have been off the station and in civilian clothes within hours. The Special Branch Officer informed me that now a full and thorough investigation would begin, and gave me instructions not to make contact with the other chaplain. He left. I returned to the church for a while then made three telephone calls: one to the station commander, one to the Chaplain-in-Chief, and one to my immediate superior the Assistant Chaplain-in-Chief. Both chaplains refused to speak to me – and continued to for weeks until the investigation was over. I spoke to the Commanding Officer's wife at their home who explained her husband was off the station for the day but had left a message for me to go to their married quarter in the evening when he returned. Over a drink he simply said: "Geoffrey, you're the best bloody chaplain I've had. I'll back you all the way, but it's completely out of my hands now." He was a caring and compassionate gentleman; an atheist as it happens.

Between the devastating morning interview and the reassuring evening balm I called on a very dear friend, Freda. The day I had initially arrived at the station – some eight months before – the out-going chaplain had driven me half-a-mile away to a broken-down farmhouse. There waiting was a bent-over ninety-two year old who had retired as a PE teacher in East London in 1945. Until a few weeks before I met her she would cycle to the RAF church twice a week for services but recently she had fallen off her bike and broken a hip, so it would be my duty to collect her and bring her to church. Under my breath I muttered: "I thought I'd come into the RAF to get away from doddering old women." Then I noticed the wicked twinkle and contented laughter lines and thought, "Perhaps it will be alright." Was ever a hunch more fulfilled? Far from being a drain on my time and energy, she became my rock in a storm; truly a God-given angel.

The next two or three months were agonizing. I was not allowed to speak with anyone about the matter within the RAF and chose not to confide in friends outside (apart from Freda), for I was still consumed with self-guilt for being who I was. The wheels of the Special Branch grind slow but sure. Eventually, I received the dreaded summons to the station commander's office. Compassionately, he explained that although every stone had been turned over – everything I had done in the RAF for five years and my life before then – nothing further could be found. I was told a decision had now been taken by the Ministry of Defence about my future. I think I can remember verbatim how the station commander put it: "The Ministry feels, for everyone's sake, it would be best if you terminated your short-service commission at the five-year point rather than the six you are contracted for. This can be done by mutual agreement by you allowing your medical category to be lowered 'for psychological reasons' to a point where you can be released on health grounds, thereby enabling you to receive your small end of service gratuity and keep your full retirement rank with no disgrace or embarrassment." It seemed a harsh sentence for asking the question: Who am I? The station commander added his personal regrets, his thanks and his good wishes.

It was a much blacker Friday than the one when I first heard about the tapped phone call: probably the darkest day in my seventy-five years. It felt an impenetrable, solid, dense black.

Three critical outcomes had now coalesced: my wife and children had fled to the in-laws; my potential lover had told me we must never meet again; and now my employers had announced I was jobless and homeless. I was stunned. It felt as though my life had suddenly stopped. There was only emptiness and numbness.

On the dark morning nine years before when I heard about my temporary rustication from King's I was given what I have metaphorically always referred to as a guardian angel in the person of the Warden of the fourth year college. He had been sensitive to how distraught I was and assured me that all would eventually be well. Now on this doubly black RAF Friday morning I knew exactly where another angel would be waiting. I drove straight to her broken-down farmhouse. Freda poured in her usual balm: an omelette made from the eggs of her own chickens with spinach and potatoes from her self-dug vegetable garden. Further unexpected disguised angels followed in quick succession. By the most extraordinary set of circumstances, totally unconnected and seemingly coincidental (which I have come over the years to recognise can often be the way the spirit moves), I was pointed towards an openly gay couple – one also a priest – living only a mile from my married quarter. They were able to listen and offer a living role model of hope – a rare find in the early 1970s. Within days I was invited to see the diocesan bishop who was nothing to do with the RAF but knew of my circumstances. He offered total acceptance with the words: "You live in my diocese and will come and work for me… and these are the names of another six diocesan bishops in England for whom you could also work" – an even rarer sign of hope in the 1970s. Gradually, helped through the appearance of these 'angels', I was able to draw on my reservoir of faith and understand the events from a totally different perspective. Was this not an invitation to take a new more honest direction in my life; a divine nudge to move in the direction of humility and away from egotistical self-dependence; the opportunity to both *ask* and *tell*? Not a time of mourning, but a time of resurrection.

I was no longer in charge of the direction my life was taking. Often I felt like a helpless piece of driftwood at the mercy of a mighty current: one moment thrust downstream by rapids, another revolving in a whirlpool, occasionally left resting precariously on a rock until a torrent washed me along. It was a time when my faith was tested to its limits. I found myself daily turning to the Books of Psalms or Job for answers and reassurance: "*... more and more are turning against me / more and more rebelling against me / more and more saying about me 'there is no help for him in his God'...*" I was testing my faith in the torrents of life and discovering I was not alone. Daily I tried to hold on in trust, keeping vigilant, noting the progression of events, unexpected encounters – the divine nudges and nods to those with eyes to see; then, intuiting the moment, take over the lead and try to act responsibly and reflectively, still letting the spirit prompt me to change pace or direction. I came to understand that it was precisely when I was not solely in charge of my life that I was truly part of a greater life.

The decision about my destiny having been made, I was at last allowed to see the Chaplain-in-Chief and his deputy. On the surface they endeavoured to show understanding – empathy even, declaring they admired my honesty. But I sensed this was a subject that caused many service chaplains personal embarrassment. I was left wondering whether I was the only chaplain with a wife and family who found himself in a predominantly same-sex organisation not entirely by accident. Twenty years later after the UK's ban on gays in the military had been lifted, all three services were advertising in *Gay Times* for recruits. As soon as the relevant legislation became law they were accepting chaplains in civil partnerships – even though most denominational churches were still having their debates. The world was moving on outside the churches.

Other interviews with two bachelor bishops (one responsible for oversight of all armed forces chaplains and the other a retired headmaster) brought forth only hostile condemnation from them. I had only sparse knowledge of their personal circumstances, but knew from my own past experience how painful it is when you are still unable to accept your own truth and a mirror is held up to you by those who have already made their personal journeys towards congruence by accepting their varying sexual orientation. My personal history during those confused years at college illustrated how my psychological defences kicked in: denial of my true identity mixed with fear and envy of others when I saw myself in their self-accepting mirror. The public humiliation of the Scottish Roman Catholic Cardinal[7] early in 2013 illustrated this poignantly when it was revealed that although he had become renowned for his public condemnation of homosexual relationships he had himself in recent years made homosexual approaches to four Roman Catholic priests. A US conservative evangelical pastor,[8] well known for his anti-gay preaching, was discovered to have been paying a masseur for gay sex. At least he had enough self-awareness to say that "I think I was partially so vehement because of my own war." Freud identified the defence of *Reaction Formation* in which anxiety-generating feelings are masked by an exaggerated reaction in the opposite direction.

By contrast, two other bishops I saw in the early 1970s – ones who took me under their wing and encouraged me to accept my true self – were able to show their genuineness and maturity by voluntarily and honestly acknowledging their own bisexuality, both adding with ironic emphasis that for the institutional church the problem had been my personal integrity. One of these – the diocesan bishop who restored my faith in myself – shared the information with me that the Bishop to the Forces (one of the ones who had given me such a hard time) had recommended to the Archbishop of Canterbury that I should be placed on the C of E's *Blacklist* – meaning that my licence to operate as a priest would be suspended. Fortunately for me, my new diocesan bishop had overruled this recommendation. No one, of course, had even mentioned to me before that such action had been proposed: such then was the lack of transparency within an institution which preaches the virtues of truth and integrity.

There remained one more formal encounter before my departure from the RAF: one of the most bizarre and aberrant actions I have ever colluded with. I was required to attend at the Ministry of Defence in London for an end of service medical examination, colloquially referred to as PULHHEEMS, an acronym for various parts of the body – Physique, Upper limbs, Lower limbs, Hearing left, Hearing right, Eyesight left, Eyesight right, Mental function, Stability – emotional. As I traversed from one consulting room to another, each specialist cursorily examined me and with a twinkle muttered the same words "A.1. Padre" – including the penultimate clinic where a flying officer psychiatric nurse assessed and passed my mental health functioning. But at the very end of the process, protected behind a large desk perched on a dais, a weasel-like bespectacled wing commander psychiatrist, embarrassingly looking away from me, stuttered: "Of course we know why you're here, Padre. Would you kindly sign this paper stating you accept that your last function on the PULHHEEMS – *Emotional Stability* – is below the service's acceptable level for service? Thank you." I felt he should have handed me my £2,300 end of service gratuity cheque there and then as a reward for making his job so easy. The cheque came a few weeks later after my demob, exactly clearing our bank overdraft. God's smile of approval, I thought.

Chapter Four

Deception

Years Thirty-five to Thirty-six
Sin is our refusal to become
who we truly are.
Michael Mayne

Away from Air Force life there were pressing issues to face and decisions to make. My parents supported me whenever I needed them to help over practical matters but feelings were never mentioned. My in-laws, although always before providing the missing emotional element, became more distant. At first we had been able to discuss the issues objectively but, understandably, as events unfolded they needed to take a different position because they were the parents of my wife and not of me. Soon it became clear that their attitude to homosexuality was as rigidly fixed as that of the majority of society and the churches: my father-in-law remained firmly within the Church's forbidden fruit ethical belief structure; my mother-in-law within the conservative establishment's traditional attitude. For the next three months my calls at the manse were short and pragmatic when collecting my daughters for their days out with me. It has taken me over thirty years to return to the towns where we had to spend those cold and wet Saturdays in museums, swimming pools, and a temporary base at an Anglican convent where we could have a sparsely furnished sitting room to ourselves to play board games, exchange news about their new school, my life, their old friends back at the RAF station and the dog which I retained. Aged three and seven they were still being told that Daddy had to work away but were probably beginning to intuit that a tug of war was beginning, even though this understanding would have been outside their full comprehension. It was a difficult pill for me to swallow after seven years of intense daily involvement in their upbringing: parting from them every fortnight was agony.

Although communication between my in-laws and me had become formalized, my wife and I were still talking regularly. We had parted with the understanding that a period of separation would give us opportunity to consider our positions and, most importantly, the position of our children. So, as the heat abated a little, we began to meet and discuss the issues more rationally. The convent, which was providing a safe haven for the children and me, also offered secure neutral ground for us to meet. The mother superior and the chaplain there were the only two who were aware of our situation. They formed part of an overarching umbrella of concerned people who held pastoral positions within the wider Church all of whom had our well-being at heart, particularly hoping the family remained together. Within an institutional ethos of obedience, deference and conformity, I complied with the proposal that I allow myself to be prayed over by the nuns, chaplain and my wife at a private service in the convent chapel. As hands were laid on me the petition was made: "that he may be made whole and heterosexuality will replace any homosexual inclinations." Now, forty years later, I ask myself how I came to submit myself to such psychological and theological travesties: "thy will be done" would have sufficed.

Since student days, once I had objectively examined the biblical, theological and ethical issues with regard to committed same-sex relationships, I had never had any difficulty in accepting equality throughout varying sexualities. Had it been only the cultural pressures I was surrounded by, even with awareness of the hurt my wife was enduring, I believe my personal integrity would have been sustained and our continued marital separation left to take its inevitable course. But the pain I was enduring through separation from my children was unbearable: I was the closest I have ever been to breaking. My wife had given me the ultimatum that unless I was one hundred per cent heterosexual she could not continue in the marriage. In response, from the grips of my self-deception, I told her that I believed I was. Had I made this response from conscious awareness I would have been guilty of perjury. But it came from the depth of my pain after separation from my daughters: my conscious awareness had been obliterated. History was repeating itself in a perverse way: whilst everything in me should have been screaming *No!* the sum of me sighed *Yes*.

The world around quickly echoed that assenting *Yes*. The chaplain and nuns of the convent rejoiced; the bishop decreed through biblical words "set your hands to the plough and do not look back"; the children were delighted that Daddy's working away time was coming to an end; my wife will have dared to begin rejoicing; my parents were relieved they could tell enquiring customers a happier story (whatever else they may have thought privately). With honesty, my parents-in-law wisely expressed caution and advised that a test period of reunion should be undertaken first. Although never stated in my presence, I think they might have been privately worried about us getting back together, particularly my mother-in-law. The set of dominoes which had previously fallen in quick succession now seemed to rise with equal rapidity. A three-month trial period of marital reunion was agreed and suitable accommodation found so that the children could continue their same schooling; temporary employment for me at a Barnardo's children's home was acquired and a proper vicar's job offered to follow. As far as the external world was concerned my career continued seamlessly and successfully. Externally and internally all manner of things now seemed to be very well indeed. Sadly, I was back to the mindset where I neither needed to ask questions nor tell anymore.

Whenever I attempted to undertake psychological or

theological reflection, all that was happening at the time really did seem to be affirming that all manner of things were well. But now, seen in retrospect, there is no doubt that the dominant narrative then was I was being driven by the joy of being with my children; the relief of being a regular family man again, accepted back into the fold of the heterosexual majority; and by the excited anticipation of starting the new job as Rector of four country parishes in the Cotswolds. The misty painful past was quickly fading. But those other things – by virtue of their very nature – could never fade away: they were omnipresent even though my pathological defences were trying to eclipse them. Years later when undertaking training in psychodynamic approaches to therapy I did not need anyone to explain what clinical *self-deception* was: I had been there – up to my neck in it.

At my Induction in June 1974 two sets of proud grandparents sat alongside the new rector's wife and daughters in their Sunday best – the youngest being briefed only to suck her dummy when dodging under the pew out of sight: we all needed to make a good impression. The parishes had expected an elderly last job dodderer and instead had been sent a thirty-five year old married retired RAF squadron leader with two young children – a normal young family. Only one other person knew any other history: a personal friend of the bishop, a wonderful woman in her late sixties who in her retirement was parochial church council secretary but during her working life was deemed one of the country's leading biblical scholars.

The Living (contract and job description in secular parlance) seemed to be a gift in every respect, with four separate parishes needing to be coaxed into one organic unit and two Church schools: challenging work for me and a nurturing community which should help restore our marriage and be an ideal place to bring up children. For the first year we all walked on eggshells, everyone behaving as perfect ladies and gentlemen in the rectory and throughout the villages. Freda – now in her mid-nineties but still active with the aid of a stick – had been willing us all well during the turbulent period and was delighted to see the family reunited, especially for the sake of the children whom she adored. She made a memorable visit during my first year, plodding up the paths of each of the four churches to inspect and say a prayer. Her visit seemed to symbolize a successful transition from the dark days to the lighter ones and apply Christendom's seal of approval. Until our respective honeymoons came to an end, we all – rector, family and parishioners – seemed to be purring harmoniously as we cautiously settled into our new routines. But there was still much to be discovered and exposed both within the walls of the rectory and the lanes of the parishes.

In the rectory masks were dropping and gradually we both began to realise that oil and water still does not mix, even though we were trying to convince ourselves, each other and the wider world that it does. Another pivotal development for me occurred after my wife insisted that my GP refer me to a consultant psychiatrist to obtain his opinion about my "psychological problem". Either serendipity or the Holy Spirit was at work, for the specialist in general psychiatry I saw at the mental health hospital in Oxford was undertaking cutting edge research in the specialised field of Varying Sexualities. Together with his wife he wrote major papers in psychiatric journals which helped to bring about the profession's U-turn regarding homosexuality as a disordered mental health condition. He summarized my ten-minute consultation: "If it is possible for you to live within your marriage you will find society will treat you more kindly. But if it isn't – and I can see it probably isn't – then I wish you well in a harsh and unforgiving world." His words were manna. He stood up and shook my hand. Once what he had said sunk in I think this became *the* deciding moment for me: the definitive moment when I knew I had become reunited with my truth and hereinafter would have strength both to *ask* and *tell* honestly.

I could now align myself with Oscar Wilde's reflections after friends had urged him to forget about his two years in prison and the implications this sentence had brought with it about who (and *what*) he was. To forget, he had remarked, would mean that he would always be haunted by an intolerable sense of disgrace, and that those things that were meant for him as much as anybody else – the beauty of the sun and moon, the pageant of the seasons, the music of daybreak and the silence of great nights, the rain falling through the leaves, or the dew creeping over the grass and making it silver – would all be tainted for him and lose their healing power and their power of communicating joy. "To regret one's own experiences is to arrest one's own development; to deny one's own experiences is to put a lie into the lips of one's own life. It is no less than a denial of the soul."

A century after Wilde's reflections, Mary Oliver (who published her first book of poetry in Ohio just as I was getting married) in *A Thousand Mornings* – "exploring the mysteries of our daily experience" – published in 2012 (some thirty-six years after I had come to my 'deciding moment') encapsulates succinctly both my long struggle through mists of denial and self-deception and my relief when I knew I was finally able to be true to myself:

Hum Hum
Oh the house of denial has thick walls
and very small windows
and whoever lives there, little by little,
will turn to stone.

In those years I did everything I could do
and I did it in the dark –
I mean, without understanding.

54

I ran away,
I ran away again.
Then, again, I ran away.

They were awfully little, those bees,
and maybe frightened,
yet unstoppably they flew on, somewhere,
to live their life.
Hum, hum, hum.

My wife and I returned to joint counselling with *Relate*, only a handful of trusted friends being aware that all was not as it appeared on the surface. During a long summer holiday at the end of our second year, in our favourite oasis on Dartmoor (where the proposal had been attempted twice, the marital honeymoon spent and healing balm applied after my year overseas), calmly and honestly, we faced and acknowledged that essentially nothing had changed: the *essence* of us each remained the same. This understanding for me was not only with regard to sexual orientation, for I realised that our differences had become such that our paths would have had to part eventually, even if I had discovered I was heterosexual and we had been able to keep the elastoplasts in position for a little longer. We returned from the holiday and began to tell family and close friends of our decision: at the end of that school term we intended to separate permanently. I vividly remember my wife returning from a visit to her parents on 1 October 1976 – two days before our twelfth wedding anniversary – informing me that her father's solicitors had advised we should move into separate bedrooms with immediate effect. My clothes were hanging in the spare bedroom wardrobe within the hour. Integrity and congruence had returned. My relief was immeasurable. Now I was on the last lap running towards my *True North*.

Probably the most helpful personal therapy I have ever

engaged in was over a period of six months, three before we parted and three after. I tried to check that the decision I had made finally to dissolve the relationship was the right one by focusing on the question: 'How does self-deception affect my relationships?' This counselling was the suggestion of my diocesan bishop who also funded it. I feel his initiative redeemed the negligent pastoral care I received fifteen years earlier when I was told that these things would go away after marriage.

Thirty years later – my masks of denial and self-deception long gone – I chose *Therapy's Light on the Church's Understanding of Varying Sexualities* as the topic for a MA Dissertation. Contributions from some thirty respondents affirmed the benefits which could be derived from effective therapeutic intervention. One Anglican Archbishop's contribution was as positive as my bishop's support had been three decades earlier:

There is still much ignorance surrounding the debate on human sexuality, especially the formation of sexual identity and the role it plays in letting people grow up into balanced adults. I do not believe the Church understands the damage it is doing in its handling of issues over sexual identity. The wisdom gained from those involved in counselling and psychotherapy could give excellent insight.

Issues of sexual identity are fundamental to our understanding of ourselves. Where these issues are unresolved the problems can be immense. For a person of faith this becomes even more an issue, especially if in a Church which gives conflicting messages about God's love, forgiveness and acceptance, while at the same time implying that to express sexual nature in any way other than a married heterosexual relationship is sinful and puts you outside the Church and its ministry. Help through counselling and psychotherapy, depending on what is appropriate, is one of the ways in which people can, and indeed have, sought help and I know of situations where this has helped enormously.

Professor Brian Thorne, a leading authority within the person-centred counselling approach to therapy, warned that in his experience therapy had always led either to departure from the Church or a radical shift in theological understanding. "It is no surprise that those for whom the Church is a security blanket (transitional object), those who, consciously or unconsciously, look to the Church for solace or social status, rarely offer themselves as willing participants in the therapeutic process." A supervising therapist who trained under him contributed a similar caution:

> The process is very painful, very complex and very long, but generally the process is life-changing. In most cases my clients are people who have become shackled from the way they have been relating with themselves and with their institutions. It is a very liberating process, but a very frightening time. It is like a place where they really can be who they really are, and to be really accepted within the confines of what's acceptable. They come to confront themselves with what they have compromised themselves with – their faith institution and their sexuality. What brings them to therapy? I think they come from an internal growing awareness, aware of pressures outside and internal tension that they want to look at. Once they reach this point, there seems to be no going back; whatever their journey is, it's never going to the same place as they have left. It was *light at the end of the tunnel* and it almost started happening by the time they started working. They want it to happen; they are on the path.

Godfrey Barrett-Lennard, who has also made a significant contribution to person-centred therapeutic theory and practice, launched his publication of *Carl Rogers' Helping System – Journey and Substance* with this wonderful definition of Therapy:

> The word 'therapy' has no verb in English, for which I am grateful; it cannot do anything to anybody, hence can better represent a process going on, observed perhaps, assisted perhaps, but not applied. The Greek noun from which therapy is derived means 'a servant', the Greek verb means 'to wait'.

Therapy does not judge, still less condemn. As Barrett-Lennard's definition indicates, the counsellor simply stands alongside, accompanying, encouraging, eliciting and challenging by asking the how, why, when and what if questions. All the respondents cited in the dissertation seemed to agree about the benefits of therapy, but also how difficult it is to convince people of those benefits enough to encourage them to engage. European cultures – British ones in particular – seem to be far more reticent to look below the masks than those on the western side of the Atlantic. One of the bishop respondents observed, "You can take a clerical – even Episcopal – horse to water, but..." It took me many visits to the client's counselling chair over a number of years before I was able to accept my true sexual orientation, let alone do something about it. Would I ever have undertaken my journey without a therapeutic buoyancy aid, I wonder?

A bizarre – yet extraordinarily symbolic – event occurred three days before the family's final parting. I returned home on the Sunday evening from conducting Evensong. The customary argument started between my wife and me, culminating with her throwing my slipper across the room and hitting her target accurately. I fell to floor in agony. Disturbed by the racket below, our ten year old daughter appeared from her bedroom. Her mother went to reassure her, explaining – tactfully – that Daddy had fallen against the rocking chair and hit his testicles. The doctor was telephoned and subsequently visited in order to check that the bruised item was not twisted. The following morning older daughter informed younger about what had happened. During morning playtime at school the infants' teacher asked the elder: "Is Daddy poorly?" "Well, sort of..." "Your sister's drawn this picture for her news and written underneath 'Daddy has hurt his right tonsil'." "Oh, it's not his tonsil; it's his testicle." Later that morning, in my role as chairman of Governors, I visited the school. Displayed on the staff notice board was my six year old's picture with teacher's red line through the word 'tonsil' and its correction written underneath. I mused: could any illustration have summarized the rectory's turmoil more succinctly?

We made the tortuous journey north on 23 December. I handed my family over to my wife's parents at a motorway service station – one to which I have never returned. The children only knew that they were going with their mother to stay with their grandparents whilst their father was working away again. The adults knew only too well the gravity of the handing-over ceremony. My parents-in-law kept their focus on practical arrangements ensuring the children were supported and protected, although underneath they must have been drowning in their whirlpool of mixed emotions – deep sadness, disappointment and anger, probably regretting they had ever asked me fifteen years before to accompany their daughter to that fateful ecumenical meeting. My wife and I parted silently. Swept along in the turbulent current of fate, I suspect neither of us quite believed what was happening: we were numb from months of emotional battering but both must have felt some relief from its cessation. Amidst all the uncertainty of what the future held for me and my acute pain as I left my daughters in that forlorn place, at least I knew I was lifting the mask of deceit. I cannot begin to know how my wife felt. Her life must have seemed like a broken vessel shattered into a hundred fragments: hopes, dreams and expectations utterly annihilated.

The bishop continued to stand alongside us all and assist wherever he could. In the mid-1970s there was still a stigma attached to divorce generally – doubled when a clergyman was involved. Without anyone being aware of the sexuality issues, to be heading towards divorced status was enough for me to make the decision to move from the parish. I had proposed to the bishop that I should accept an offer to take up a director's post with a secular charity. Before making any final decision he asked me first to attend a month's specialised training for senior clergy at St George's College, Windsor Castle. Without mentioning any family dissolution I announced publically that I had been asked to undertake this training and whilst I was doing so my family would stay with my wife's parents. My devious intention was that at the end of the month I would slip quietly away without having to face people when the divorce was announced. Higher forces – heavenly as well as earthly I believe – had other intentions. When travelling on a remote gated road in brilliant winter sunshine on Christmas morning, two days after our family separation, between the eight o'clock communion service in one church and the nine o'clock in another, I had an overwhelming conviction – gut intuition – that I was running away like a pathetic coward. I loved the place and the work, why leave? The very soil seemed to be shrieking: *Stay*. These questions continued to drill into me whilst I was away on what transpired to be one of the most challenging and inspirational pieces of training I have undertaken. At the end of the course I called on the bishop and shared my reactions. "Silly boy," he exclaimed, "why do you think I sent you on the course? Now go back to the parishes and visit each of the eight churchwardens this evening. Tell them the truth about the divorce and that you and I want you to stay in post as long as they are happy." The next day the churchwardens unanimously reported they wanted me to stay. The bishop issued an amended decree: "Now it's a different plough and different direction but the same instructions. Get on with it with my blessing."

Chapter Five

Realisation

Years Thirty-seven to Forty-three
And in the book I read:
God is love. But lifting
my head, I do not find it
so. Shall I return

to my book and, between
print, wander an air
heavy with the scent
of this one word? Or not trust

language, only the blows that
life gives me, wearing them
like those red tokens with which
an agreement is sealed?
RS Thomas

My ministry in the Cotswold villages continued for a further six years: years which were not without considerable challenges both professionally and personally, yet were also rewarding and fulfilling. It was a time when I identified with greater clarity something that I had sensed throughout theological college years and during the following decade as I served my apprenticeship as an ordained and married man. I began to separate theological chaff from wheat: the *wheat* which seemed to belong to a life of faith (essential meaning and purpose); and the *chaff* which seemed more to comprise a similar bundle of distorted ecclesiological and confused psychological baggage to that which brought my father to his succinct conclusion: "They're all a lot of hypocrites." On the surface what seemed to be expected of me in a rector's role contained less of the former and more of the latter, which was a dangerous temptation for me because it could easily play into that familiar life script – the long social haul out of trade into professional classes. Fortunately my other life challenge – sexual identity – was beginning to be exposed and could prove to be an antidote to any social climbing temptation. To succeed in the 1970s in North Oxfordshire as a conventional Anglican clergyman required a thoroughly heterosexual pedigree – or at least a heterosexual mask. I was beginning to discover that a divorced clergyman was just about passable (useful even to fill a vacant space at the dinner table when a divorced or widowed woman might need a companion), but not the sort of divorced clergyman that my integrity was increasingly urging me to reveal. These truths too had to be learned the hard way as the next six years unfolded.

Two close friends (lay readers) – the retired Old Testament scholar and a father of four my own age who later became an ordained head teacher – encouraged and upheld me as we began the daunting task of gently coaxing four congregations away from what sometimes appeared to be their fossilized feudal format into becoming faith communities which might have something more relevant to offer the rapidly changing demography of their rural villages during the last quarter of the twentieth century. It appeared that the wider Church's reforming spirit during the 1960s and early 1970s had passed them by. The theological reservoir they drew water from seemed to belong more to the nineteenth than twentieth century for they appeared never to have heard of biblical criticism, the ecumenical movement, liturgical revision, or Synodical governance and lay participation. We set our six hands to the plough to face prejudices around class division and gender discrimination; to question preconceptions about allocation of time, talents and finances; to encourage outward-looking, accepting and inclusive attitudes rather than ones which could be interpreted as judgemental or condemnatory.

Three incidents may give a flavour of the challenges we were facing. The first was when I preached a sermon and illustrated that Sunday's bible reading – Jesus' various injunctions about humility (the first coming last, choosing the lower seat, etc) – by recalling an incident from my RAF days in the Oman when an ad hoc communion service was held in a desert outback. The commanding officer had instructed that padded armchairs be placed in a front row for commissioned officers, upright carver chairs in the next for non-commissioned officers and wooden benches at the rear for other ranks. I arrived early and repositioned the chairs in a semi-circle deliberately mixing up the various categories. Different ranks sat wherever there was a space as they arrived and the service proceeded and concluded without comment by anyone: there was only an overpowering and respectful silence. Amongst the congregation I have profound memories of middle-aged Mercenaries with battle-scarred faces and hands – professional soldiers hired to serve in a foreign army – who probably had not attended formal worship for a decade or more kneeling humbly on the sand to receive their bread and wine. Having just knelt to receive his communion in the Oxfordshire church where I was preaching, a retired RAF Wing Commander parishioner accosted me at the church door: "Padre – you are a disgrace to the service for saying what you did about the commanding officer and the chairs."

Soon after this incident, in one of the other villages, the wife of a much-respected retired army colonel and county councillor died. Her husband asked if the choir could sing at her funeral. That church's tradition at funerals was to position the coffin between the normally empty choir stalls, but as there would be young children (including my eight year old daughter) within a few inches of the coffin I suggested to the undertaker that on this occasion it might be better to position the coffin in front of the high altar on the other side of the sanctuary rails away from the children. Within days the gossip came back: "Oh, now we know what sort of rector he's going to be: the nobs will get into the sanctuary and we'll have to stay down below." I countered the rumour head-on the following Sunday, repeating the story about the RAF chairs I had told in the other village.

The third incident occurred in my fourth year when battle lines were firmly established between the old guard defending the status quo, and an increasing number who were advocating changes. The bishop and I had proposed a scheme which would formally combine the four parishes into one autonomous unit. Three parishes backed the scheme; one opposed it strongly. A joint meeting chaired by the bishop's representative was called. It became one of many occasions when I was ashamed to have any association with institutionalized religion. An entrenched member of the status quo lobby rounded on me with venom: "You come here disrespectfully addressing us all by our Christian names..." I take no pride in my sarcastic response: "I thought we were a Christian community"; silence and humility would have clothed me more fittingly. It was a sad and painful evening. But at least colours had now been publically nailed to the mast and we could begin a process of mutual understanding, healing and compromise. There were many good and honest people who had faithfully said their prayers and cherished their hopes as generations passed over the centuries within a socio-logical system which at its best would ensure that the strong or materially fortunate looked out for the weak or underprivileged, even though there still lingered some of the less healthy vestiges of patronage where a rigid class structure ensured that upstairs and downstairs only met during Christmas carol singing expeditions or at the summer village fete. A powerful memory remains of a time I preached the same sermon to congregations in each of the villages. Locked in their churchs' four vestry safes were antique silver communion chalices – one dating back to years in the reign of Elizabeth I. Touching the chalices I mused: "Think of the many lips which have made contact with this same silver... across social and generational boundaries; in times of war and peace, famine and plenty; friends and enemies within and without of wedlock... many of your great, great, great, great grandparents treading across the same soil to reach the same buildings and touch the same silver as our lips will touch today."

So, the months and years passed – the common parish round. We tried to go on telling the story of the God we believed had brought us all to these Oxfordshire parishes and was present at the heart of our village communities: the God of our muddles and messes as well as our successes and joys. Inevitably, a few for whom our contributions became too disturbing (or threatening) faded into the background, but many more who had previously ignored or rejected the Church seemed to come out of the woodwork and tiptoe towards us seeking deeper relevance for their lives and answers to the questions they were asking about human existence. We hoped we were gradually becoming an ad hoc collection of people who were on a humble journey of faith exploration rather than any better-than-thou-holy-huddle of churchgoers.

It was not only through the challenges of a rural ministry that my faith was being tested: years of painful separation from my children lay ahead. We were all – children, parents and grandparents – still coming to terms with the reality of the marriage dissolution. Formal divorce proceedings were underway; my wife, supported by her parents, was working out her future as a single parent; I was losing myself in work, compensating for the vacuum an absent family had left behind. Before my wife and I parted we agreed that it would be explained to the children that we were not living together anymore, but that both parents loved them and would always look after them. We agreed that the gay issue would only be explained when we were able to tell them together. Frankly, looking back from what I now know (and deal with professionally all the time) we could have handled things much better – particularly my own collusion in a conspiracy of silence by not letting the children know what was really going on. My former parents-in-law's well-intended parenting style was inclined to shield children from painful reality, so they made a priority of keeping the children busy and happy. I was still riddled with embarrassment about the gay implications and found it impossible to broach the subject. My former wife was still shattered by shock from what had happened and the implications of her new status. We all lavished attention and love on the children, but no one would tell them the truth. Children are not stupid – and certainly not ours; their intuition communicated without need for words or explanations; they knew that two and two did not add up to the five they counted.

Within a few months of the separation their mother accepted the offer of a residential post in the South of England and moved there with the children. I visited soon afterwards and when putting the youngest to bed she asked: "Daddy, when are the doctors going to make you better?" I realised instantly what must have been said and quickly assured her I was not ill, just a little different, and would always be there to love and look after her. I asked her mother what had happened and referred to our commitment to only mention the gay implications when we were together. She explained that the children's incessant questioning had left her with no option. Although disappointed – annoyed because it was *me* whose business this was – I realised in the given circumstances she really had no option but answer their question when they asked it as best she could.

Although unknown to me at the time, my eldest daughter had found the information that we would never again live together as a family devastating. It was over a decade later – a period when she was living and working with me – when she was able to talk about it. Apparently she had been so upset after her mother had told her that she locked herself in her room for over twenty-four hours. I was horrified when she told me this. I remember leaving my chair, falling to my knees and sobbing tears of remorse in her lap. The consequences of the trauma she sustained at such a crucial developmental age as ten will never fully be known.

The problem was that relationships were so fractured for us that joint conversations were not a viable proposition: far from any healing process beginning, positions were polarizing and bitterness setting in. As their mother's depression deepened they all soon returned to live with the grandparents, and communication between me and the adults was conducted on a business basis only. I was not even informed when the children's mother was admitted for a number of weeks to a psychiatric hospital. I had to make a formal application to the court for access arrangements to be changed. A complicated legal battle began which affirmed the contribution I made to parenting, resulting in the judge adjusting arrangements in my favour. It was all totally horrible: a terrible and catastrophic mess. How a harmonious wider familial set of relationships could degenerate into such bitterness was tragic and would take many years to heal.

Under the new terms for childcare my daughters spent more time at half-term and the main school holidays living with me. I had desperately wanted to abandon those cold and artificial Saturdays out with Daddy. Even to this day I feel I can recognise a father having access time with his children from two hundred yards away: it replays smarting memory tracks for me, accompanied by an aching yank in my stomach. We settled down to a regular pattern where the children would travel between the two bases. I could never refer to where they lived with their mother being their home because of the implication that my house was their holiday venue. This was my problem and not theirs, for clearly their new base in the North of England was the home where they attended school, undertook extramural activities and developed friendships: it was their growing-up milieu. I made sure they retained a bedroom each in my house; developed their old friendships in the village; had a second Christmas or birthday celebration. I was still partly in denial of reality; but it betrays the emotional torment I too was enduring. The last thing I wanted to become was a sugar daddy. I wanted to reclaim my part in their parenting – the good and the bad bits. I desperately missed attending parents' evenings, sports days, concerts and plays at school; I longed to run them hither and thither as their social lives expanded; I ached to be part of the agonizing daily disciplining process as homework had to be completed on time and restrictions be placed on the hour they came home: all the silly everyday every family growing-up hassles and tensions. I was quickly learning that true fulfilment comes from – and true love urges you to contribute to – the mundane, pragmatic and challenging building blocks in a child's development.

It was not only me who was on an experiential learning curve. My daughters, who were far less emotionally equipped to sustain these complexities during their formative years than me in my mature adult ones, were far more vulnerable, particularly during their adolescence when they had to cope with their own internal turmoil. They can only properly speak for themselves, but my agony then was multiplied as I sensed their confusion and anguish. They were being given so many mixed messages. When talked about in the North I was described somewhere along the continuum from being sinful-cum-criminal to sick-and-to-be-pitied: when they were staying with me I appeared to be a respected figure within the community, a responsible father and capable home manager. I was increasingly aware that my very existence had become both an inconvenience and an embarrassment to my former in-laws and ex-wife. They had even suggested I should join a newly formed monastery. In so many ways I felt my parenting role was being subsumed and rights being taken away: the word 'kidnapped' was never far from my lips when asked how my daughters were. Yet I was equally aware that everyone could only experience the situation from their own particular standpoint: we were all bruised and hurting from the family's new configuration. The children's grandparents had already had their turn of parenting and would now have been expecting a very different involvement as grandparents: instead they had to play the part of auxiliary parents with all the tensions that teenage parenting brings. My ex-wife was clearly struggling to cope with her situation and I can well understand her disappointment and resentment given the systemic realities she found herself engulfed in. The pressures inflicted by the complex dynamics of her own family of origin, followed by the evolving reality of her marriage, are classic ingredients for a major depression. For us all it was a time of confusion and incredulity, but for the girls – despite being surrounded by so much love – it must often have been a time of darkness and despair.

Reflecting back now, during that first divorced year (and I still shudder when I have to tick the 'divorced' box on official questionnaires) I developed an almost pathological paranoia about my status. Although I threw myself into my work I managed – heaven knows how – to do it without ever going into shops or other public places in the centre of the village in which I lived unless I had a professional reason to do so: I was ashamed to show my social face. And this was only because of the divorced status; only an inner circle of close friends knew about the other thing. I knew that it was a reflection on the prevailing social and geographical attitude to clergy and divorce, but there was still a large part of my psyche which remained ill at ease even though I thought I was personally resolved and integrated.

Over time the overwhelming acceptance of friends and colleagues helped the guilt and shame to subside. I probably made more close friends during this period than at any other time in my life: people both from within church circles (kindred spirits who shared my fantasy that we sell the medieval buildings, pitch camp in a broken-down barn and start again to live a simple life of faith), and many outside the Church (kindred spirits who shared almost the same fantasy but slow-pedalled on faith and majored on alternative lifestyles – with alcohol). The village seemed to attract thinking and caring people who were searching for simplicity and genuineness. My friends, both within and outside the Church, were usually trying to release themselves from the shackles of convention, image and status; looking outside themselves to make a contribution towards healing an ever more greedy and selfish world. These friends were a great antidote for my gradually fading upwardly mobile life script and became confidants who helped me accept my true divorced gay self.

In my own household, with only Radio Four and a Clumber spaniel for company, I was experiencing for the second time how it felt to live alone. Whether there is an innate instinct implanted within us to walk this earth two by two, or whether it is a process of programming we acquire from the cultures in which we grow up, I am not sure: possibly both. Just as I had had the teenage fantasy about the young man I first fell in love with – that we would each one day marry and live in adjacent connecting houses – so, from the moment I knew my marriage was going to dissolve, I assumed I would meet a compatible male soulmate and begin a committed responsible life as a single unit. I more than assumed it: I believed this would transpire: it seemed only natural after everything that had happened to me – my just desserts and God's reward. I was not surprised therefore that an unexpected encounter occurred – only amazed at the precision timing.

Shortly before the fateful motorway journey north with my family I met someone who has impacted upon my life more than any other person. Within a very few hours like seemed to recognise like. The more layers of our respective histories and beliefs we unpeeled the more we found staggering synchronicity. The one exception was that whilst I was about to become divorced he was married. Apart from this all the preconditions for compatible coupledom seemed to have been met: we were attracted to each other to a degree neither of us had known before and had more than sufficient in common to know we wanted to develop a relationship. It took very little time for us each to acknowledge we had fallen in love and knew this was no fleeting teenage fantasy: indeed, it has been a relationship which has survived the test of time, albeit developing in a very different way to how I hoped it might.

For the next six years we were able to enjoy the closest of friendships, professionally and personally. But from the flames of our mutual love we came to accept that priority had to be given to existing personal commitments – especially the needs and interests of children – not just our own desires: in the midst of the fire we were being challenged to understand that selfless love, rather than singular self-interest, is the fulcrum of authentic prayer. As people of faith we needed to accept that our ultimate destiny lay in hands other than our own, learning the sacrificial truths of a hard and harsh gospel. But as human beings – flesh and blood – it has not been easy. Over nearly forty years, ebbing and flowing between flames and embers, and despite many attempts to dowse the fire, it has proved to be a love which is hard to extinguish: the ashes seem always to retain a small embryonic spark. I know psychologically I have found it extremely difficult to accept the reality of our situation – my familiar self-deception battle between fantasy and reality. There has been perennial wrestling within the three driving influences of my inner life – my head, my heart and my gut: logic and reason, emotion and dreams, instinct and intuition have battled against each other. I have found I can easily revert to my hidden default position and allow my dominant personal defence mechanism – *repression* – to take over the driving seat. To borrow

Yeats' metaphor and Eliot's words: (it has been) *the foul rag and bone shop of the heart;*[9] (and become) *the passage which we did not take... the door we never opened.*[10]

Through this, more than any other life experience, I have come to understand that even though two people may have the same object in view or experience the same sensation they always look, think and feel through the eyes, head and heart which are unique to their own particular circumstances. Even though they may dance the one dance, through their separate and unique sequence of movements and steps, they engage with the world in different ways. As a first century poet put it *what is food for one person may be bitter poison to another.*[11] In our case, each of us has partaken of food and poison in equal portion in order to reach our different integrities. Now, as we have had to go – or rather *chosen* – our separate ways, our choreographies have developed very different routines. Systemic circumstances (partners, friends, lifestyles, career choices, geographical locations and economic circumstances) have shaped us differently to the extent that we now inhabit different worlds. To those observing from outside the relationship these developments must suggest that the preconditions for compatible coupledom no longer exist, and with my head I realise this is true. But the wisdom of pragmatism can easily be tempted by the determined powerhouse of the heart as it whispers when *"love bids you welcome... so you should sit and eat."*[12] The question 'How does self-delusion affect my relationships?' is one I must ask throughout my lifetime, not just during that post-marriage six-month period of psychotherapy.

Throughout those eight extraordinary Oxfordshire years, despite the complexities and challenges of church, children and relationship, I felt I was in the right place at the right time. I was surrounded by interesting kindred spirits who I loved and who supported me. There was still work to do in the parishes, and in the wider local area where I was gradually becoming known. The children had settled to their regular time with me and had many local people welcoming and supporting them: I could almost dare to think it might become their second home. Geographically, it could have hardly been a better place to live, especially if you preferred country to town, as I did. I held the Living of the parish, which meant I had security of tenure until I was seventy. Why even think of moving?

I was forty-three years old, entering what some would describe as my prime working time. I was aware that two of my immediate predecessors had stayed in their parishes, respectively, for thirty-seven and fifty-two years. Comfortable as it was, did I want to fossilize in north Oxfordshire, too? I began to consider my future. I no longer had to make my geographical location a priority because of choice of schools, or consider environmental factors being suitable for my family to live in. I was a free agent: even my trusted dog had just died. My developing theological and political position was moving to the left, so that the environs of the Chipping Norton Set and the Heythrop Hunt were ceasing to be as attractive as they were when I was a married, medically-retired squadron leader. I was quickly realising that I could only be fulfilled and gain integrity by finding a professional job which was compatible with these developments. I was also only too mindful of the strain my fully requited but unresolved relationship was putting upon me. As I struggled to make a decision, the combined conscious and unconscious strands of the motives and reasons for considering a move seemed to exceed the complexity of any Gordian knot and would prove to need divine intervention to unravel.

I shared most of my thinking with my bishop and we agreed to keep our eyes out for a challenging inner city post. Within a short time the post of Warden of one of the old University Settlements in East London was brought to my attention. The brief details available looked interesting enough for me to consider an exploratory visit to the terrain – for I had hardly ever been further east than the Tower of London before. During the children's Easter break, without mentioning why we were penetrating into East London (but using the excuse after a request from my youngest that she would love a denim skirt and that the East End was the best place to find one), we ventured forth. All I wanted to do was drive around the streets and get a feel for the place. I returned promptly with my tail between my legs and with the overwhelming feeling that I could not leave the Cotswolds for *this*: it seemed totally alien. Close that book.

When I returned my daughters to their mother I was asked to carry their suitcases to their bedroom. There I could not help notice wallpaper hanging off the walls caused by quite severe damp. Driving back down the motorway this chilling image drilled into me. I knew my church salary would not enable me to increase my maintenance allowance (I was already overextended because of it) and yet felt I just had to increase my income in order to contribute more. I remembered the post of Warden was advertised with accommodation and a third more remuneration than my clergyman's salary. I knew what I had to do – another Damascene moment. Obstacles in the way again fell like dominoes. My interview was on Maundy Thursday (an annual day when many things of Passiontide importance in my life seem to happen). Like the resurrection after Good Friday, there was an agonizing wait until the appointment letter fell on to the rectory doormat on Easter Tuesday. I had six months to tell everyone, prepare, and move.

It was just before our decision to end the marriage that my ninety-five year old angel, Freda, died. She would have been devastated to see the family dissolve. I returned to take her simple and happy funeral. During the months she had been such a support to me; although the cottage and its contents were humble in every other respect, I had fallen to the temptation once or twice of mentioning how attractive her walnut roll-top desk was. A week or so after the funeral her executor phoned to say she had left me something in her will and could I call to see him about it. I would be disingenuous if I did not acknowledge my slight hope that it might be that desk, for I had never had a proper desk before. When I arrived he told me, "She has mentioned that she has left you her most precious possession" – and handed me her much used and much loved copy of The Jerusalem Bible. He must have noticed my tears welling-up, but would have been ignorant of the humbling irony behind them.

My final church service in the Cotswolds, a glorious church-packed occasion, made up for all those previous painful endings. It concluded as I knelt silently alone in front of the high altar expressing my gratitude to God who had led me to this remote corner eight years ago. Hidden away somewhere in the church the melodious voices of children from two Church of England primary schools which had been an important part of my ministry rang out. Accompanied by a single guitar they sang, *"Let me take your hand and lead you through the streets of London..."* I floated out of church on a river of tears – not just my own. My one great regret was that my daughters were unable to be there: an omission redeemed eighteen years later when they were able to accompany me to Buckingham Palace. But much water had to flow down the Thames from its source in Oxfordshire to my new location near the Royal Docks before then.

I needed the first pint of beer from the local brewery poured for me at the merry reception in the primary school hall which followed the service. Speeches and presentations began. The churchwardens unveiled my farewell gift – an oak roll-top desk. No one but I and God knew the inner story about roll-top desks and the treasured bible; no one knew I longed for a desk; no one knew the depth of my gratitude to God behind the tears that welled up again. One dear old lady, a strip of damp wallpaper, a tattered bible and a roll-top desk had joined the throng of signs and signals which had helped to rekindle my faith over the years. When observed as solitary items they could easily be dismissed as insignificant coincidences, but when arriving in clusters at significant moments of my life they have reignited smouldering embers of faith.

People outside faith will baulk in incredulity at such an association. The gift of a roll-top desk: does God really look after his own in this way in a world where so many die from starvation, treatable disease and war? The significance for me was not the *gift* of the desk – not that I had been favoured by God – but that it had joined the long list of *signs and signals*: what the rector to whom I first communicated my thoughts about ordination called in his reply postcard "divine nudges and nods"; and the German Jesuit Karl Rahner more eloquently expanded in a prayer:[13]

> What can I say to you, my God? Shall I collect together all the words that praise your holy name? Shall I give you all the names of this world, you, the Unnameable? Shall I call you, "God of my life, meaning of my existence, hallowing of my acts, my journey's end, bitterness of my bitter hours, home of my loneliness, you my most reassured happiness?" Shall I say: "Creator, Sustainer, Pardoner, Near One, Distant One, Incomprehensible One, God both of flowers and stars, God of the gentle wind and of terrible battles, Wisdom, Power, Loyalty and Truthfulness, Eternity and Infinity, you the All-Merciful, you the Just One, you Love itself"?

From my own faith experience I want to add: "God of the roll-top desk, damp wallpaper, tattered bible and – particularly – little old lady", and to join the author of the Book of Hebrews in affirming that I have been "surrounded by so many witnesses in a great cloud on every side, that I, too, should throw off everything that hinders me... and keep running steadily in the race I have started."[14]

RS Thomas encapsulates perfectly the theology that was being forged out of my own life experience as I discovered that the presence of an incarnational God is to be discerned in the stuff of the universe. In one of his two poems entitled *Emerging* he speaks of a world in which not only "matter is the scaffolding of spirit", but in which the holy is revealed in the ordinary; and that the ordinary is far more extraordinary than we think:[15]

Emerging

Well, I said, better to wait
for him on some peninsula
of the spirit. Surely for one
with patience he will happen by
once in a while. It was the heart
spoke. The mind, sceptical as always
of the anthropomorphisms
of the fancy, knew he must be put together
like a poem or a composition
in music, that what he conforms to
is art. A promontory is a bare
place; no God leans down
out of the air to take the hand
extended to him. The generations have
watched there
in vain. We are beginning to see
now it is matter is the scaffolding
of spirit: that the poem emerges
from morphemes and phonemes; that
as form in sculpture is the prisoner
of the hard rock, so in everyday life
it is the plain facts and natural happenings
that conceal God and reveal him to us
little by little under the mind's tooling.

Little did I know as I left for the next stage of my life's journey that the 'peninsula' to which Thomas refers was the Lleyn Peninsula in North Wales where he lived and ministered for a decade, and would two decades hence become the place where I too would live and work for a decade, and where I would discover even more about "matter being the scaffolding of spirit".

Chapter Six

Fulfilment

Years Forty-four to Sixty-one
What is the meaning of life?
The great revelation had never come.
The great revelation perhaps never did come.
Instead there were little daily miracles, illuminations,
matches struck unexpectedly in the dark.
Virginia Woolf

The new race for me began on 1 October 1982. My mother lovingly helped me pack my belongings into the removal men's tea chests, clean the rectory in preparation for its new occupants and polish my car until it was fit for the nation's capital. She told me how pleased she was that I had this exciting new appointment, without betraying her own bereft inner sadness about me going to live a hundred miles away. My focus had long been on the new challenge ahead. From the thorough private research I had undertaken before I applied for the job and from what I had gleaned during the gruelling day's interview, I had realised that even though the organisation was at a low point in its distinguished ninety-three year history it had enormous potential. Currently, there was little relevant activity delivering the charity's objective: To obey the Christian imperative by supporting the local poor and needy. There was a healthy endowment of nearly £1 million; an impressive collection of individual and grant-making trust supporters; two very substantial buildings; a separate fifteen acres of playing fields in the heart of the London Borough of Newham plus sixty acres of farmland on the edge of Hainault Forest only half an hour's drive away. All property and sites were owned with freehold.

A further unexpected challenge had inadvertently presented itself during the interview procedure. Sitting in-between two long-standing board members during the informal lunch I asked an innocent historical question. One of them answered: "The great period of expansion was between 1923 and 1961 when the bulk of the capital was donated to acquire prestigious buildings and substantial land. Then we had the scandal." With unshocked tone I enquired, "Scandal?" "When the great Warden who'd built it all up for thirty-eight years was tried at the Old Bailey." "Old Bailey?" I continued to probe, my eyes probably growing larger. "Yes, for offences with young men, I'm afraid, but that's all in the past. We've sorted out those disgusting goings-on now…" followed by many tut-tuts and expressions of shock and disapproval by trustees within earshot. I remember projecting a silent prayer towards the heavens: Interesting – why have I been sent here?

My first day in post as Warden of Mansfield House University Settlement started with a crash. The acting chairman of the Board of Trustees, on discovering my predecessor was a few days late in vacating the warden's accommodation, kindly invited me to stay at his not insubstantial Mayfair residence. At dinner on the first evening he explained that he and his wife did not do breakfast but he would bring me a tray in the morning. At seven on the dot a knock came at my bedroom door. As he entered he tripped on a rug and sent the laden breakfast tray flying across the room. Many years later he told me that from that first day he had been impressed because I was more concerned about his well-being than my stained working clothes. And so I was, for a seventy-three year old knight of the realm spreadeagled on the floor was a frightening sight – until I found he was unharmed. It was a fortuitous beginning for it allowed the three of us to establish a mutual relationship of trust: a foundation which was to prove invaluable for the tempestuous journey ahead.

The central assembly room of the Settlement's classic 1920s art deco main building was modelled on the Grand Saloon of the Queen Mary Liner, designed by the same architect. Shortly after my arrival I knelt on its sprung ballroom floor before the Bishop of Chelmsford as he prayed for my future ministry and handed me his formal Licence: *We, being satisfied of the soundness of your morals, learning and knowledge in Holy Scripture DO, by these presents, give and grant to you our Licence or Faculty under the Provisions of Section 2(1) of the Extra-Parochial Ministry Measure, 1967... etc.* Legally, the Settlement had nothing to do with the Church of England; it was a non-denominational charitable Christian organisation founded by Mansfield College Oxford when it was a Congregational Theological College. However, my immediate predecessor had been appointed on a half-time basis twenty years earlier to help recovery from the scandal as he was also the local parish priest and area dean and, importantly, as far as everyone could see successfully married. As his predecessor – the Warden with the scandal – had also been a lay reader there had been a strong association with the C of E for over half a century. Understandably, most people assumed the Settlement was part of the established church.

For me there was far deeper personal significance in asking the Bishop to formally License me as Warden. At that stage of my psychological and theological development I was unable to cut my ecclesiastical umbilical cord: ordination as a priest (or having the *status* of a clergyman?) had become an essential part of my personal identity. I applied for the new post because it seemed to offer the opportunity to express my faith in a relevant way, not (consciously) because I wanted to leave parish ministry. Now, seen from the perspective of how I have developed theologically and psychologically over the succeeding three decades, I believe the transition then from parochial to extra-parochial ministry was of pivotal significance. It was an epiphany moment for me even if I was not fully conscious of it then.

Although never my daily attire any longer, the clerical collar remained my protective armour on selective occasions during the first year. Gradually, as I grew in confidence and integrity, I was able to see how I was using it more as a crutch. The collar's abandonment seemed to mirror my dance with the institutional church. Since ordination I had been discovering that much of what the Church appeared to present to the outside world by its dogma and practice seemed irrelevant – bad religion – whilst its faith's (Christianity's) powerful insights and beliefs – good religion – seldom seemed to find accurate or adequate expression. In my role as a parish priest I had been required to act out many of the misrepresentations. Now, painfully aware of these distortions, I could have mistaken the *church* for the *faith* and easily thrown the baby out with the bath water. I had to remind myself of my first spiritual promptings during my late teens and early twenties, and the great cloud of witnesses that led to this new phase in my faith journey. These experiences were no mirages and needed no demythologising: they were neither misapprehensions nor psychological defences. Neither did I need to collude with the conditioning which I felt had always been applied by the institutional church by looking upon vocational promptings as their institution's exclusive preserve: a priest forever after the order of Melchizedek was not necessarily synonymous with possessing a formal Bishop's Licence. In this new post – this continuation of my vocation – there was only one commitment to make: the one I made silently alone on my second day in post when visiting the Settlement's empty country site – *Here I am. I don't know why. Use me as you will for two years or twenty*. It turned out to be eighteen.

The institution which had been placed in my care seemed to have strayed a long way from the radical vision of its founding fathers in 1889. Coming five years after the advent of the first university settlement – Toynbee Hall – it stood within one of the most deprived communities in the UK. In an era before the introduction of the welfare state, Mansfield pioneered soup kitchens, mother and baby clinics, a Poor Man's Lawyer scheme (precursor to Legal Aid) and numerous other initiatives to alleviate poverty and deprivation. Oxford undergraduates would reside (settle) for a period of time in East London to live and work alongside the local community. They were acting in true nonconformist tradition by spurning ecclesiastical trappings – social status and conformity – and were trying to live simply in line with what they saw as the teachings and example of Jesus Christ. They incorporated these principles in the Settlement's foundation document.

Although strong in principle and resolve, these early pioneers lacked material backing. Mansfield was a poor hall of Oxford University, not even a college in its own right until 1995. But, from the 1920s onwards, through the endeavours of the new (honorary) Warden who came with personal wealth and high societal connections, the Settlement could expand and flourish. Under his stewardship it became a prestigious Boys' and Men's Club, claiming to be the biggest and best in Europe. A world-renowned architect was employed; eminent public figures like George Bernard Shaw and Noel Coward were recruited to demonstrate their support; official visits were made by King George VI and Ministers of State; the grand and the good throughout the land became regular donors. They must have been happy years with amazing achievements, particularly – but not exclusively – in the domain of sporting excellence. Local people were deeply appreciative of what they had been given and proud of their own achievements.

But with the success and exuberance came a profound change in culture and focus in the institution's philanthropic endeavours. Membership of the Boys' and Men's Club – which perhaps was the single new factor which most symbolized the change in culture – dominated and seems to have become ninety per cent of the Settlement's involvement with the local community. Worthy and relevant as it was, many would say also exclusive and elitist: there were hardly any activities for women and girls, and vast categories of growing social deprivation were being left untouched. Then after thirty-eight years of glory came the scandal, which was much publicized in the national press. The Warden had been knighted for his good works in East London. As well as his position at the Settlement he held a minor cabinet post as Conservative Member of Parliament and had recently been nominated to become a life peer. The day before *The Times* published the exposé the Settlement had a huge number of annual subscribers; within a couple of weeks it had dropped to a mere handful.

After the fall from grace the organisation adopted a policy of keeping its head below the parapet until national memories faded. Locally the community seemed more forgiving, perhaps realising they had gained far more than they had lost. They had a different attitude to such human frailty. For the next twenty years the Settlement seemed to live off the better parts of its historical reputation and enjoy its physical assets. The new part-time Warden, whose primary job was being a parish priest, rural dean and local councillor, continued as titular head, his permanent dog collar, dark suit and wedding ring providing the Settlement's respectability. East Londoners – ever renowned for their initiative and ingenuity – made good use of the facilities, which remained almost exclusively for males and increasingly those who were achieving through a wide range of sports. Meanwhile the borough was rapidly and radically changing demographically: many of the white indigenous community were moving out into leafy Essex and being replaced by a wide variety of ethnic minorities.

From the outset I had let it be known that I did not intend to change anything for at least a year: my task during this time was to look, listen and learn. What I found confirmed my pre-appointment conclusions that there were both amazing resources of plant and reputation to draw upon, and escalating local social deprivation requiring those resources. But I had not previously realised just how great the gap was between potential and the present reality of the Settlement's underuse of resources – sometimes inappropriate use. At the end of the first twelve months I presented a damning report to the Board of Trustees about the state of their organisation, how some of its current functioning might contravene charitable law, and tried to outline a vision for the future. I suggested that we had to cease being principally a privileged sporting facility for a small minority of achieving males and return to the only corporate raison d'être we were legally and morally allowed to have. Soon after my appointment the Chairman of the Trustees had quietly said to me, "If you hear a rumour that it might have been suggested to your predecessor that he retire early, it is more than a rumour." Although not realising the extent of the malaise, I think trustees understood that radical reform was necessary.

Radical though my proposals were, by comparison with what was to follow within the next few years they were fairly modest – cosmetic even. We set objectives to raise £1 million for building renovation; become inclusive of ethnic minorities; undertake a major feasibility study about the underused country site; try to sell the now defunct but potentially extremely valuable land which had been a sports ground; take advantage of a new central government unemployment initiative; innovate a health and welfare programme for people with learning difficulties and mental health challenges; and become inclusive of both genders in all activities. Having met in an open session with our own senior staff members, other local voluntary sector leaders and borough council officers (all invited to contribute to the discussion) the Board of Trustees unanimously accepted the report and gave me carte blanche to execute the proposals.

I bought a smart new grey herringbone sports jacket to help raise the £1 million. It proved to be the wrong choice: we plateaued at about £300,000. Slowly it dawned on me that despite all these developments the underlying culture was not changing. The London famous boxing club, the nationally famous table tennis club and strong judo section all claimed squatters' rights and continued to occupy the majority of a four-storey twenty thousand square foot building. The hundred-men-strong rugby club which had commandeered the whole of the sixty-acre country site, with their open all hours bar passing £10K of alcohol through the Settlement's accounts each year, had major plans to turn farm buildings into a superior clubhouse. Whilst every member had moved out to more affluent Essex, the site's trust deed clearly stated that this facility had to be used only by the poor and needy from East London. The dominant sporting interests with their exclusive male elitist dominance were still in the driving seat: the Board's new initiatives were seen as threatening additions. The old guard made it clear to the new arrivals that they were not welcome. Reflecting whilst away from my daily involvement, I began to see (as I had seen in my marriage) that oil and water would never mix.

On my first day back from holiday I had an unexpected visit from two local authority officials. They had each made unannounced formal inspections of the art deco building during my absence. Both officers acknowledged that we were trying to comply with current legislation by the £1m appeal to update facilities, but first the fire officer then the environmental health officer told me that if we did not comply with statutory regulations with regard to fire and health safety by midnight they would have no option but to bring me – as Chief Executive and Company Secretary – before the magistrate by noon the next day. Angels in disguise, I wondered?

Shortly before this bombshell I had acquired two significant new staff members. The first was a recently retired main board director of an international food production company renowned for closing down many plants and factories across the world and still coming out smelling of roses from union meetings – as his company chairman described him when recommending him as our new Appeal Director. The second addition was somewhat different. Out of the blue I had received a telephone call from a young man who was working for a local Christian organisation and was involved in a number of cutting edge social justice initiatives regionally and nationally. He was looking for a new job. The Settlement had just been awarded a grant for a year's salary for me to appoint a personal assistant. He fitted the bill and was duly appointed to work closely with the new appeal director. Both brought radical vision and energy: a great blessing for me.

The combination of limited response to the appeal (few funding sources seemed to want to perpetuate elitist sports in an outdated building, despite our new vision); irreconcilable cultural strands within the Settlement (new wine in old skins syndrome); and dangerous financial pressures from our revenue budget (because the obsolete projects were unable to attract external funding) were bringing things to crisis point. During the visit of the two local authority officers I glimpsed a solution – perhaps the only viable and ethical solution – and asked them to put their ultimatums in writing.

I gave my two new staff members the task of gathering statistics to support the various options which might be open to us. Their combined expertise along with their new objective eyes produced a powerful and succinct report. If we kept going the way we were we would be heading for bankruptcy. It was not difficult for me to present a convincing case at an emergency meeting of the Board. Visionary trustees quickly grasped that a root and branch approach was now necessary; more cautious ones worried about the financial implications and concluded it was the safest route to take. On a dark autumn evening the decision was made to obey the local authority officers' injunction and close the principal building – including all the activities undertaken in it – with immediate effect, and begin a sale procedure. The elitist sporting groups would be assisted in establishing themselves as independent units; all staff would be made redundant, except me, the caretaker and a newly appointed manager for the country site. My new personal assistant and the appeal director would stay on for a time-limited period.

We were effectively closing down the whole organisation as it had been running for half a century, and returning to its earlier roots. It helped to have received just before the closure decision had to be taken, first, a superb feasibility study for the sixty-acre country site, and then an independent external evaluation of the Settlement's overall position describing the vision for the development of the country site to become an environmental, farming and outdoor activity personal development residential centre as being the potential *jewel in the Settlement's crown*. It was this vision that persuaded the Board to take such a radical step and has without question over the last thirty years proved to be the right decision to take.

Controversial policymaking – the Board's responsibility – when the relevant issues at stake are so clear is comparatively easy; implementation of policy – my responsibility – was another matter. There was little sleep for me the night after the trustees' emergency meeting. I had three dozen staff to make redundant the next day; copious funders and supporters to bring on board; press to deal with; a building to sell which had been unexpectedly Grade II listed a few weeks earlier resulting in stringent change of use restrictions being applied. Once the devastating news became public the old guard contacted politicians, press and their unions; protest marches were organised to the town hall; obscene personal threats directed at me were painted on the rugby club's walls; not surprisingly, everything hit the fan. I had much sympathy with the protesters, for it was not the fault of staff or service users that things had gone so awry. I did my best for twelve months to help heal the corporate bruises and assist individuals and groups to move forward into new occupations or locations. The implementation of plans for the future could wait: too many people were hurting. Close friends asked me how I managed to cope through this turbulent and painful time. My response was heartfelt. As with my divorce and the changes which had to be made in the rural parishes, when you glimpse truth you can only go towards it. And in any case, nothing will ever be as painful for me as facing the reality of my sexuality in my particular situation then and the loss of daily contact with my children. Those historic experiences seemed to have prepared me for the challenges I was now facing.

Over the next few years the Settlement introduced a variety of innovative programmes that tried to fulfil the vision of our founding fathers. Under an umbrella strip-line of *Poverty Never Sleeps*, more than half our projects focused on children and young people who were at risk: detached street youth work and after-school care supported those damaged by neglect; residential or day visits to our country farm and outdoor activity site allowed the natural environment to help change disruptive habits and heal psychological wounds. In total, some five thousand youngsters each year passed through our hands. Alongside the initiatives with young people, other new programmes for adults were gradually introduced (managed directly by the Settlement or through sister tenant organisations) ranging from support for people living with HIV/AIDS; those with mental health challenges; victims of crime or domestic violence; the frail, lonely or elderly; various unemployment schemes; mediation projects; citizens' organising – an initiative bringing together diverse local groups across the wealth and social spectrum. We strove to ensure that not only did our work fill gaps in provision left by statutory authorities and other voluntary organisations, but also that it truly addressed the needs of local people who were most vulnerable and marginalized.

After all the upheaval of closing down the old and beginning the new Mansfield, and the challenges involved in being open about my own situation, I was soon to be tested even more intensely on the battlefield of faith and sexuality. Many members of the expanding staff team at our country base were finding spiritual nourishment through a conventional evangelical faith which traditionally questioned acceptance of sexual diversity. The advent of an HIV/AIDS project supporting some hundred gay men at our city base, and at the same time the adoption of a comprehensive equal opportunities policy throughout the Settlement, plus knowledge of my and one or two other staff members' open same-sex partnerships, brought tension within the wider staff team. Healing came only over months of open and honest exchanges – monthly full staff meetings, residential training events, team-building fun days away. Then myths were dispelled and gradually mutual respect for one another's integrity and dedication to work was acknowledged. For me healing was complete when at a national evangelical conference, in front of a couple of hundred voluntary sector workers, an American speaker staged a role play where he acted as counsellor to a young man who was wrestling with his gay identity. The usual 'love the person, condemn the act' theology was advanced. I stood up during question time, declared my ordained status and openly gay relationship, asking only that those present – particularly the younger ones – knew that what they had just witnessed was not the only belief and practice of people of faith. Some dozen members of the Mansfield outdoor centre staff team rose as one body from their seats on the far side of the hall – led by one of my daughters who was then running our farm unit – walked over and hugged me. On another occasion I was summoned to the borough town hall and told by a senior executive that our grant was being withdrawn. I discovered that it had been assumed that we, like another local Christian

Settlement, were disenfranchising gay and Muslim people. It gave me great pleasure to disabuse the local authority officer by exposing her to my personal and our institutional circumstances, evidencing numerous gay and ethnic minority service users, staff and volunteers. The grant was reinstalled.

When I left Oxfordshire friends gave me a delightful etching of a nineteenth century working man looking perplexed in front of a signpost which pointed in two directions, one to West Ham, the other to East Ham – the exact terrain I was heading for. The man holds two leashes attached to dogs which are pulling him in opposite directions. At the time of my departure the picture symbolized for me the painful triangular relationship I had wrestled with for six years, for underneath was the text *I do perceive here a divided duty*.[16] But as my engagement with the Settlement deepened the picture and text became symbolic of other realities. First, I saw my familiar self-portrait moving upwardly through the class strata being reflected in the whole raison d'être of the Settlement Movement: how the fallout from everyone's random accidents of birth was now at the centre of my daily work. My professional raison d'être was to help bridge the gap and heal some of the tragic results from life's socio-economic game of chance. I could easily find myself on the same day dining at one of St James's gentlemen's clubs promoting our work after having spent a number of hours with service users at the Settlement. They were different worlds. Which one did I belong in? Throughout its history you can trace how those who were heading-up the Settlement's work have straddled this continuum, some living their lives predominantly in the society of Central or West London and occasionally visiting the East (even though they might live there), others making the migration in reverse. Like the man with his two dogs, perhaps I too was born to bear the strain in the middle?

But there was a deeper struggle coming into focus and disturbing me: another not unfamiliar challenge. Did not the demands of that hard and harsh gospel – the radical Jesus teaching and example – require not only sacrifice in my intimate relationships (as I had already accepted), but a far greater personal commitment than any political swing from right to left might achieve? Did it not invite a root and branch deepening of belief and change in lifestyle; a total reframing which might be incompatible with my present persona? The shadow cast by my father's comments about the Church's hypocrisy was still penetrating deeper crevices of my marrow, even if outwardly it might have appeared that I was contaminated by upwardly mobile progression which had required me to conform to the expectations of 'establishmentarianism'. Again, I seemed to stand in the middle, bearing the tension, moving neither westwards nor eastwards. Perhaps I really should start believing that this was where I belonged?

The Anglican Society of St Francis, a religious order of friars, had a base a few hundred yards away from Mansfield for almost the same length of time as the Settlement had been in the area. The Franciscan focus is to embrace poverty as a gift from God and live community life in the world serving the poor. The strands of our two institutions had interwoven and separated many times over the decades – a pattern which continued during my time at Mansfield. Inevitably the degree of collaboration varied as individuals came and went. On many occasions they restored me in both body and soul. I am only sorry I did not always fully appreciate their presence as one of God's gifts for, when they were being true to their calling, they provided an antidote whenever I drifted away from a simple Nazarene[17] faith or started any upwardly mobile ascent.

During Margaret Thatcher's 1980s the East/West tug of war intensified. A damning report from the Archbishop of Canterbury's Commission on Urban Priority Areas highlighted the gaps in society: growing unemployment; demise of traditional industries; increase in institutional racism; inadequate housing; lack of investment in educational and social services – similar manifestations to those outlined in the 1883 Parliamentary Report on London Poverty and in the Settlement's foundation literature six years after that. In its early years Mansfield had been more radical in its social policy. It was the only institution in London to give a platform to Keir Hardie (regarded as one of the primary founders of the Labour Party) when he came down from Scotland. From the 1930s onwards, under the influence of its distinguished Warden, it became increasingly seen as a philanthropic organisation of the concerned middle and upper classes. I remember the response of our Chairman of Trustees when I wrote a document about *The Disadvantages of Paternalism within Society*: "What's wrong with paternalism?" I was experiencing the answer daily. When I took up the Warden's mantle in 1982 I made it one of my first jobs to observe a meeting of my new local council – the London Borough of Newham, combining the former East Ham and West Ham boroughs. This was very different to the municipalities I had been used to in the Cotswolds. It was probably the first time I felt my arms stretched on the cross of the East/West signpost. Never again did I enter the town hall wearing a grey suit and dog collar!

But my arms were stretched most during the last two-thirds of my time at Mansfield by tensions that lay at a deeper, more fundamental, level. By drawing attention to growing inequalities within society and prioritizing those who were disadvantaged, Mansfield may have remained loyal to the intentions of the founding fathers of both the Settlement and of the Christian faith, but it ran against the grain of a growing secular and materialistic society. By the end of the 1980s it felt as though a new generation was being infected by a cancer where self-interest and self-advancement were eroding the altruism of former generations. I realised it was seeping over from the corporate and public sectors nationwide into our organisation at every level. A few trustees were suggesting we might adopt a bonus policy for remuneration (a proposal I rejected outright); some staff colleagues – not many – seemed to be prioritizing their own rights and rewards over those of service users; a number of funders appeared to be more focused on the benefits which they could derive by sponsoring our work, albeit always carefully wrapped up in a more philanthropic package. Two external agencies brought home to me how different the East/West worlds were. When a leading advertising agency helped us prepare for our centenary year I learnt much about the importance of creating the right image and about packaging and marketing – and accepted their gift in kind. But it always haunted me that this would not have been the way my Franciscan brothers and sisters – let alone Jesus – would have chosen. The Settlement had a prestigious firm of West End lawyers who in past years had undertaken decades of work pro bono. A new generation of partners in the post-Thatcher era could not understand me raising questions about charges in excess of £300 per hour. From every direction I felt *Get on your bike* was declaring war on *Poverty never sleeps*. Somehow I had to try to stay holding firmly on to the two straining leashes at the East/West signpost; try to remain as true as I could to Jesus' simple message; try – even against the promptings of my personal life script – not to be seduced by the many allures which tempted my personal ego. I know I did not always succeed.

Years spent in preparation for Holy Orders seemed a long way from the duties and responsibilities I found myself involved in at Mansfield: learning and knowledge of Holy Scripture – as my Licensing document to this post had ascribed – seemed a long way from skills to read a set of accounts, produce and implement strategic social policies, raise £000s and manage a budget, lead a staff team and guide Boards of Trustees. It took me some while to accept without guilt that I was fulfilling the priestly vocation to which I still felt called by interpreting and implementing the

Objectives from Mansfield's 1889 Memorandum of Association in a way that was relevant for the Settlement's second century:

(i) *To promote the religion of Jesus Christ in its most comprehensive meaning, but so that special attention shall be given to its social action and aims.*

(ii) *To provide philanthropic services... to enquire into the condition of the working classes and the destitute, and to carry out plans and schemes to promote their welfare.*

Yet, perhaps it was precisely those years spent preparing for Holy Orders that began to open my eyes to the real message of Jesus of Nazareth, and helped me to sift through the chaff and wheat of religion. At Mansfield I believe I found my professional *True North*. I was given the opportunity to turn faith into action. To borrow Michael Mayne's words:[18]

... a vision of a world in which people are more concerned with giving than with having, with sharing than with possessing, with serving than with being served; where each is valued for what he or she *is* rather than what they *have*; where the narrow loyalties of class or race or tradition or party are of less weight than the solidarity of the human race created in God's likeness; and where in areas of conflict and violence forgiveness and reconciliation have been proved to be the most powerful of all weapons.

The single incident which probably rejoiced my heart most during those halcyon eighteen years – sadly one I did not witness personally – happened some six months after we had expelled the rugby club from our country site. Half a dozen rugby players turned up unannounced and told the manager of the newly established residential centre they wanted their barbecue back. Apparently they had constructed a very superior one and forgotten to take it with them. They were escorted down to the swimming pool on a sunny afternoon where two or three dozen children and young people with very severe physical and developmental difficulties were preparing a barbecue. My colleague simply said: "Is that the one? Please help yourself." With one voice the others said: "No. Sorry. We now see what you're doing. We understand. Please keep it as a gift from us." Was God ever more manifested, I asked myself?

The new Appeal Director who had helped bring about the Settlement's radical reorientation, although a failure at raising the £1 million (we used to tease him), was quickly recognised as someone who could make a substantial ongoing contribution to the Settlement's work and was invited to join the Board, becoming its next Chairman. He stood alongside me through all the institutional changes which followed. I learnt much from him about strategy and management, and we became close friends. The other new staff member appointed at the same time came alongside me in a different way. Within six months of working together we recognised that we were mutually attracted and started a happy personal partnership. We were never happier than when sharing our vision for the Settlement's revival, wrestling with policy and its implementation.

But it was still only the mid-1980s – early days for gay emancipation. We were both entangled in our different ways in institutional Christianity with all that that implied for same-sex relationships at that time, and the Settlement's corporate scars from the scandal had not completely healed during the two and a half decades that had elapsed. A number of different searchlights seemed to be shining on our relationship simultaneously. We returned from our first holiday away together resolved to work out the next career move for my partner, and asked to see his trusted Baptist minister together in order to brainstorm various possibilities. To our surprise the Baptist minister announced he also had an agenda to discuss and confronted us by saying that whilst we were away he had heard a rumour that we were a homosexual couple. We each replied with our own personal stories, summarized as *So what*? The following day in a meeting with four local leading clergy of various denominations this new information was shared by the minister, resulting in my bishop being informed of the situation. The bishop invited me to join him for afternoon tea at the House of Lords and after hearing my story said he had no problem but as President of the Settlement thought I should discuss the matter with my Chairman: if the Chairman was also happy everything would be fine.

It transpired that the Chairman was away in the Mediterranean sailing for a couple of months but his wife, who had become a good friend too, listened to my story. "Oh dear," she said, "he thinks highly of you but this is a subject he has great difficulty with" (and shared confidential family infor-mation about why this might be). After she had spoken to him on my behalf and he had then spoken with my bishop he told me he accepted my situation as long as my partner in due course moved on to a new job – something which he was planning to do in any case. The mutual respect and trust the chairman, his wife and I had established since the breakfast tray crash, combined with his family's pertinent circumstances, no doubt had helped this positive outcome.

My partner and I were back on track and enjoyed six happy years together. Some people suggested we became something of a role model for same-sex relationships within the local voluntary sector, particularly parts associated with the churches. We were never militant campaigners for the gay cause (as we became for Women's Ordination), but equally never hid our relationship. We just got on with everyday chores and responsi-bilities, living and working happily together. He taught me a lot about social justice issues, the priesthood of all believers and introduced me to the music of Tracy Chapman and Barbra Streisand. One Christmas we went together to the annual Clergy Chapter Dinner when the invitation had been addressed to clergy and their wives. Nothing was said, but the following year invitations came addressed to clergy and their partners. I remember us attending with friends the Wimbledon Whole Foods Barn Dance where we both partnered lonely women all evening until the last dance, which was announced as being the *Gay Gordons*. Then we thought we should dance together. When the dance-caller noticed us he simply changed his instructions from "the gentleman does this and the lady does that" to "the person on the inside does this and the person on the outside does that". Throughout the six years we acted, and as far as I was aware were invariably treated, as a normal committed couple.

It is always difficult to assess what keeps a relationship together and what allows it to drift or split apart. Having had the privilege of working as a *Relate* and a *Primary Care General Practice* counsellor and having listened to many hundreds of other people's stories during the last ten years, I have almost come to the conclusion that 'if it works it works, if it doesn't it doesn't'. Sometimes couples you think had their relationships made in heaven fall apart and those you think should never work hobble along, even flourish. In making these observations I am probably projecting not a little of my own experiences. I realise that the painful time I went through in my close relationship in Oxfordshire must have been in the mix of motives that brought me to London. I also realise that, whatever its provenance, the 'two by two' instinct has been – still is – a strong part of my DNA (interestingly, confirmed by ancient wisdom from the Enneagram personality system which assigns me the descriptor of 'The Lover'). I was thrilled to begin the new happy relationship when I first came to London. It had a large component of that wise Prayer Book purpose for marriage, *the mutual society, help and comfort that the one ought to have for the other*: an ingredient which rightly has been elevated from third to first place in modern liturgical versions. The relationship really did work well for both of us. But I think for me – and I can only speak for myself – I was so deeply affected by what had recently happened to me I was unable to commit myself to the depth the relationship deserved. It would not be appropriate to discuss this or any other of my personal relationships in more detail through a public medium, but I think I can say that although in retrospect it has proved – for both our sakes – to have been right to move on, the way in which I terminated things was unnecessarily hurtful to my partner. This is one of many decisions in my life which, if I could go back over it again, I would choose to do differently. He deserved better.

I chose to move on to a relationship which was charged in its early days with strong electricity for both of us. For me, at the beginning it was reminiscent of my experience in Oxfordshire (hence I think the potency of my attraction), but I was soon to discover the relationship had none of the necessary components for long-term compatible coupledom. I was middle-aged – then fifty-one – yet acted as a lovesick teenager swept off his feet by someone much younger who I am sure loved me, but had a very large unresolved agenda from his past. It all went horribly wrong after the first six months and took a further eighteen months to unravel and completely dissolve. I became deeply bruised through the experience: some have said it affected very considerably my ability to move on appropriately to a new compatible relationship. Fortunately one of my daughters was living with me during the last painful months and the other was working for the Settlement. They gave me enormous support over a very difficult time.

There followed a period of what I have often described as "wound licking" which, for the next three years, took the form of a caring and mutual friendship. As far as I can make sense of what took place (or did *not*), I and another man each had our emotional needs met through the liaison, but our needs were different in nature, even though they might have been felt with the same intensity. I think therefore to some extent we had reciprocal satisfaction, albeit for each of us different in kind. For my friend it was a supportive platonic friendship which helped him through a difficult transitional period; for me, although being that too, it was also a potential erotic relationship which I hoped might have been reciprocated as more than just a friendship. Yet at some level of awareness which I was mostly not conscious of then, I have a suspicion that that was the very reason I chose this particular liaison, stayed with it and gained much sustenance from it for so long: precisely because it was never going to be requited. It has been one of my life's greatest conundrums. I well remember the evening when I finally accepted the reality of the situation and let go of my internal fantasy that one day the magic fairy would make it all well and we two would live blissfully together. We were sharing a meal with one of my oldest friends – a psychiatrist as it happens – who knew us both well. In vino veritas, the ramifications of this unusual friendship/relationship were being dissected and the friend with whom I was infatuated tried to help me close the gap between fantasy and reality. After experiencing my resistance to accepting facts he shrieked: "*You and I will never be lovers.*" I was stunned and silent. The message had finally got home. The atmosphere was unbelievably charged with emotional energy. Our psychiatrist friend rose from the table and selected a suitable CD of emotionally charged music. For the next couple of hours of steady drinking, with hardly exchanging a word, we each took our turn choosing a similar timbre of dramatic music. Gradually the intensity of emotions subsided; we staggered to our respective beds; the dawn came and we all enjoyed a cheerful breakfast. For me a new, fantasy free, day had begun.

Andrew Sullivan,[19] when describing his coming-out as a gay man at the age of twenty-three, went on to observe:

Perhaps this is a homosexual privilege: for many heterosexuals, the pleasures of intimacy and sexuality are stumbled
upon gradually when young; for many homosexuals the
entire experience can come at once, when an adult, eclipsing
everything, humiliating the developed person's sense of
equilibrium, infantilizing and liberating at the same time.

I have always been aware that my emotional development had in
effect been stunted because of the repression which had gone on
well into my adult life. Had things been different when I was
young – society's understanding in the 1950s and my own
awareness and maturity – in all probability I would have gone
through a number of attempts at intimate relationships between
the ages of, say, fifteen to twenty-two, before establishing a
longer-term more committed one. Many gay people have made
the same reflection to me. Like teenagers who repress their
normal adolescent inclination to rebel can find themselves
having a latent experience of rebellion in mid-life, so gay people
can find themselves having to make up for lost time by undertaking some experimentation before settling down. I found I was
sometimes going through this catching-up process during the
years when I was not in a committed relationship. All I need to
record here is that I tried to undertake it responsibly, mutually
and respectfully with a few men, nearly all of whom I shared
more interests with than just the comfort and pleasure of
physical intimacy. I have no moral scruples about reciprocal sex
between consenting adults, but once you have swum at depths
where two equally attracted minds and hearts find their ultimate
union in mutual coupling, sex without love is a poor substitute.
In my experience, after the soothing balm of summer
Mediterranean waters, a winter plunge into the North Sea brings
only momentary relief and limited pleasure.

Whilst the Mansfield liner was navigating its ocean U-turn and I was exploring my new world, my family life was simultaneously undertaking its own reconfiguration – and was about to hit an iceberg. My daughters, now able to travel by themselves, had established regular visits during school holidays and half-terms. London must have been an exciting alternative to northern provincial life for a teenager, and they were always given a warm welcome by my colleagues and friends. In particular, my new partner seemed to be relating well with them without anything being spelt out specifically about the nature of our relationship: we appeared to be one happy cluster when we were together. On one visit, my younger daughter, then aged thirteen, had come for a few days by herself when my mother was staying. After supper my partner and daughter seemed to be taking an inordinate amount of time to complete the washing-up. When they joined us in the sitting room I intuitively sensed something significant must have transpired in the kitchen. Only later was I told by my partner that my daughter had asked him if he and I were lovers, to which he had given an honest answer. Without discussion, I announced at breakfast that my daughter and I would be going out for the morning. The conversation which had taken place the evening before was one which I should have initiated as soon as the new relationship began; I had ducked my responsibility and left the issue to take its own course. However, no harm seemed to have been done. Our morning outing had gone well and my daughter returned happily to join her sister, mother and grandparents in Devon. What hot news she had to share with the others!

Three weeks later – joining the other black Fridays – three hammer blows came on the same day. First, a formal communication from my wife's solicitors enclosing a handwritten letter from my daughter to me stating that she never wanted to see me again, and quoting relevant bible texts to evidence the wickedness of homosexuality. Paradoxically, it had only been during her recent visit that she had complained to me that her mother was going through an evangelical phase and was making her attend weekly boring bible study groups. The solicitor's letter stated that because I was living with another man they were starting proceedings to ensure that my daughter's visits could only take place either at my mother's house or when my mother was visiting my house. Then, later in the day, I received a telephone summons from the acting diocesan bishop stating that he had received a disturbing letter from my former wife enclosing copies of the letter from my daughter to me and the solicitor's letter. He would like to see me the following day. The most shattering blow came in the early evening when my mother phoned in tears unable to speak. She had received copies of all the correspondence from the solicitors. I told her I would be with her within three hours. I phoned two of my close friends – my trusted former GP and male lay reader – from the village where I had ministered for eight years, and they were sitting with my mother within minutes, staying until my partner and I arrived. My mother, who knew the facts and accepted my partner, was assured by us all that this silly matter would soon pass. We made the return hundred-mile journey the next morning in order for me to keep my afternoon appointment with the bishop.

When I explained to him that the retired diocesan bishop, in conjunction with the Chairman of my trustees, had given approval with regard to my relationship, I was accused of being a liar. I drove straight to our neighbouring Franciscan Friary and asked the Guardian, another good friend and colleague, if he could obtain through the Franciscan network a contact telephone number for the retired bishop who was visiting his daughter in Australia. Within a couple of hours I had the number, made the phone call, and was told by the retired bishop, "Leave it to me, I'll sort him out."

There followed a very painful period when I had no contact from my younger daughter but regular contact with the older one because she was over the age of sixteen and could act as she chose. Within a few months my younger daughter, through the mediation of her sister and without her mother knowing, made contact and for a further six months or so we remained closely in touch, sometimes meeting without her mother knowing. Eventually visits were openly resumed.

During the period when we were not supposed to be in contact I received a distraught telephone call around four o'clock on a Friday afternoon from my younger daughter. She had left home for school in the morning after having had a major row with her mother. She told me she did not intend to go home. It placed me in a very difficult position, for neither her mother nor grandparents knew she was in touch with me and I did not want to break the trust of my daughters. I was about to conduct a training weekend for 18–19 year olds who were beginning a gap year assisting in various parishes around the country as part of their faith exploration. We were literally beginning the introductory session as the phone call came in. I explained what had happened to my colleagues and the group, asked for their thoughts and prayers, and caught the next train out of King's Cross. Arriving mid-evening I found a distraught fifteen year old and took her to a local hotel. I doubt if the proprietor believed my booking for two single rooms was for father and daughter; but more importantly, by the morning she had agreed to return home. Looking back from three decades later, this may well have been the pivotal time that changed my daughters' relationships with their two parents. Since then they have always been – and remain – two of my closest friends.

When both daughters were respectively somewhere between their seventeenth and eighteenth birthdays more or less the same cameo was re-enacted. On each occasion daughter and father were enjoying a meal out reflecting on our complicated family circumstances through their post-adolescence understanding. As I went over familiar territory, each daughter made similar observations: "Well, Dad, I suppose really you shouldn't have been married." Each time it was followed by a pondering silence, a wry smile, a sip of wine, and then, "I'm glad you were!" They both spent increasingly more time with me during their early adult years. The eldest came to work with me on our new farm project for seven years after graduating at agricultural college; the youngest came to live with me when she started an art foundation course in London and again, with her partner, after graduating at university. The close friends with whom I shared my agony over my separation from the children during those turbulent days in Oxfordshire, and others who had known us as a family together since the children were born, used to reassure me: "You have always been a loving and supporting father. Continue keeping close. Believe in your love. It will come right in the end." They were right.

There was a sequel to my contretemps with the bishop who was looking after the interregnum before a new diocesan was appointed. Despite the fact that he had been assured by his retired senior that approval had been given for my relationship, unknown to me, as soon as the new appointment was made he wrote to warn the new bishop of the irregular situation which would be waiting for him. When the appointment was publicly announced Mansfield trustees asked me to invite the new man to become our President (following his predecessor). I made sure two letters were on his desk the day he took up office: a personal one from me requesting an appointment and a formal one from the Board inviting him to be President.

The Settlement had recently entered into a partnership with a national church scheme for youngsters who wanted to offer their services as volunteers in local parishes – effectively a gap year experience. Mansfield provided accommodation and helped with the training. My partner had recently been made coordinator of the project and also wrote to the new bishop asking for an appointment to tell him about the scheme. Because a large sum of money was being invested by the church organisation towards a major refurbishment of one of Mansfield's buildings, it was proposed to mark the beginning of the new venture with an act of worship, inviting the new bishop to preside. He undertook this as one of his first public engagements, witnessing the promises from the representatives of the two organisations – my partner and me – and then processing around the building blessing each area, including the self-contained flat on the top floor which we occupied. My partner and I had devised the whole event and written the order of service together without conscious awareness at the time of any parallels with gay blessings!

After a couple of weeks I was invited to visit the bishop and spent a happy hour explaining my life's history first – including the various goings-on with his predecessors – and telling him about Mansfield's work. He listened attentively and wished me well but made no further comment. Two or three weeks later my partner was called in. He told his story and talked about his work. The bishop told him how impressed he had been by my openness and integrity, and confided how he had received this warning letter from the assistant bishop adding: "Before I left that evening for your service of blessing my chaplain informed me 'that is where *that* Geoffrey Hooper is'." He thanked my partner for coming and wished him well. The next day a formal letter arrived from the bishop addressed to me saying how pleased he would be to accept the trustees' invitation to become the Settlement's President. From then on, as a matter of courtesy, I went to see him once a year to bring him up to date with our work. 'Other matters' were never mentioned. I hold happy memories of our times together, most of which seemed to be spent with him talking about the demands of his job. On my final visit, before he retired, he thanked me for my support of him during the years.

Eighteen years is a very long time to be in any one job – today almost unheard of. At two or three points during my time at Mansfield I seriously considered a change. Like all major life decisions, it is probably impossible to unravel the Gordian knot of motives – boredom, ambition, fear, personal/partner/family circumstances, and a raft of unconscious stuff too. After the Settlement's centenary celebrations in 1989, when the major organisational changes were achieved, I applied for the post of Chief Executive of a very well-established branch of the YMCA. It was an ambitious job – more prestige, more responsibility and what I perceived would be greater security and stimulation from being part of a worldwide network. After a rigorous selection process I received a telephone call to say that I had been successful; but before the confirmation letter arrived, I was called in for a further meeting with four senior trustees. "This is very embarrassing, but we have heard that you are in a relationship with another man and, although we are an equal opportunities organisation and we personally have no problem over the issue, we feel that established supporters here would not quite be ready... etc." By some discreet detective work I discovered that their informant had been my evangelical area bishop who "just thought they should have this information as the YMCA was a Christian organisation." It was long before national gay anti-discrimination laws had been passed (and in any case the House of Bishops had secretly negotiated a get-out clause with regard to the employment of clergy), so there was little I could do. But I smiled when I recalled tales told by my oldest school friend about his gay exploits in the baths of the New York, Central London and various other YMCAs.

A similar scenario was repeated two years later shortly after I had started my new partnership. By then I was more settled to the task of consolidating the work of Mansfield and happy to continue in post, but was looking for new challenges and also (before the time I saw more clearly that my vocation to ordination was finding authentic expression at Mansfield) feeling I should re-engage with parochial ministry. I think there was an unconscious motive too, for my partner – with whom I was still smitten – wanted to move westwards where his job was located. A prestigious central London parish was advertising for a part-time priest to initiate new links with the local community. I negotiated with my trustees who were happy for me to continue in post at the Settlement on a part-time basis whilst undertaking this new work, living half-time at each geographical location. I was interviewed and appointed. My partner and I went to inspect the flat that was on offer and meet the two churchwardens. I was called back for a further interview with the vicar who explained that there was no problem about me being gay but his church-wardens were not sure that the parish would be happy to have us living in an *openly* gay relationship. He made reference to his predecessor – by then a very senior bishop – who had recently featured in the national press over his ambiguous remarks about his own sexual orientation "and we don't want to fan the flames for him". The vicar added – stroking the cat on his lap affection-ately: "I'm probably lucky because I've never had a committed relationship myself so the issue has never arisen." The irony with this situation was that it was one of the most gay-renowned parishes in the Church of England, and had been well before the years I was at theological college. It was an open secret that the majority of the clergy and congregation were 'card-carrying members', albeit most of them carefully closeted. So sad. So hypocritical.

Another sequence of these now familiar patterns occurred not long before I finally left Mansfield (of which I will say more), only this time less transparent and more underhand. I had been asked by a clergyman in a very senior position to apply for the post of Warden of a long-established Retreat Centre in order to revitalize it and establish alternative pastoral approaches. The new evangelical diocesan bishop (generally known to be anti-gay) and his enthusiastic wife were heading-up the interviews. After the appointment process was complete, it transpired that the two favoured candidates were a lesbian priest (who I knew well) and me. Some explanation was given for neither of us being appointed even though we had both passed all the hoops. Unfortunately, when he was giving me his version of my results the bishop did not know that I had already been given the accurate facts by my friend the senior colleague. I had caught the bishop out being rather 'economical with the truth'. There was a trail of sad stories around about his contrasting attitude to gay clergy to those of his two predecessors (the bishops who had been supportive of my relationship and of the Settlement's work in their role as Presidents) and – as it has transpired – to his two successors.

This last attempt to discover the door to my future came as one of a number of false (or failed) trails which I followed during 1999/2000. I felt I had achieved as much as I could at Mansfield and, having been through a number of landmines both in the Church and wider voluntary sector myself, wondered if I could offer support to those who were still battling – as one friend put it succinctly – clapped-out clergy and other voluntary sector leaders. This intuitive urge was nothing new: it seemed to have been creeping up on me for a number of years, but there always seemed other priorities that I had to focus on, both within and outside Mansfield.

Not least was my involvement with the umbrella national organisation for Settlements *BASSAC*.[20] Although it often took me away from the Settlement – especially during two years when I was Chair – it enabled Mansfield to make a contribution on a wider canvas. I am not a particularly political animal and was more than content to leave the Chief Executive – a former Baptist minister who had been a good friend for a decade – to inspire the organisation with his vision and implement radical policies through his strong leadership. His contribution was immeasurable. He transformed the organisation and took it to a completely different tier in both the national political and voluntary sector strata. Tragically, after a short illness, he died in office when he was at the peak of his career. It left a gaping hole. I was able to offer pastoral support during this difficult period and oversee the appointment of a successor – which proved to be a particularly challenging task. But there were other complications. Whilst in London, with both the British Association and International Federation,[21] the Chief Executive was joyfully accepted as an openly gay man in a happy partnership: at the weekends he lived with his Baptist minister wife and family in the provinces. They all knew what the score was, but the two lives were kept in separate boxes without wider circles at either end knowing the real situation until the funeral and a very complicated memorial service. It was another occasion when I felt I was in the right place at the right time being used for the right purpose. It joined what was by then a long list of serendipitous events which flamed the embers whenever my faith was flagging.

The promptings to move from Mansfield became more dominant. I chanced upon an article about Atsitsa on the Greek island of Syros, how "its simplicity and intimate connection with nature offered timeless detachment from the outside world and an atmosphere that enables everyone to venture into unchartered waters." I had heard about it before and thought it looked interesting, but when a single telephone call late on a Sunday evening offered me the last place available in a few days' time on a two-week adventure, and those two weeks happened to be the only ones I could have managed during the next six months, the green light shone. I committed myself to attending a workshop in the mornings (the first week African Drumming, second African Dance); treated the afternoons as a solitary retreat walking in isolated countryside with a positive focus on what my next step in life should be; and the evenings relaxed socially amongst fifty or so fellow explorers. It worked! My head, heart and gut became reconnected and I returned home with a clear understanding that I should move on from Mansfield – and made this announcement to the Trustees at their next meeting giving them fifteen months' notice. Within days of returning I bought my own bongo and started to drum out my unique rhythm.

Preparing to leave Mansfield consumed most of my energy for the next twelve months. It focused on bringing about a compatible merger with a similar local Christian charity which had been working in the borough for as long as Mansfield. In brief summary – which does not do justice to the complexities involved – the other charity was property and cash rich; we were land and project rich. Both Boards of Trustees and external stake-holders welcomed the proposal; my staff colleagues, whilst seeing the pragmatic wisdom, were suspicious of the impending cultural change and some decided to jump ship. But under the new configuration *the jewel in Mansfield's crown* – the trans-formed rural resource – was released to develop its independent identity with a separate Licence. It has forged forward more than fulfilling the vision I had always cherished. During the year my mother died peacefully a month before her ninetieth birthday, but sadly just missing the letter from Downing Street announcing the award of my MBE. I used any spare energy discerning what was going to happen to me next.

The conviction I came away with from Atsitsa was as strong as the message I had gained two decades earlier from the damp wallpaper: I had to move on. To what, for what and where was yet unknown and had to be discovered. The process of discerning right choices at such pivotal moments in our lives is a complex one. By then I was sufficiently psychologically aware to know that varying personality types – by whatever co-mixture of nature and nurture such characteristics develop – will approach the discerning process from different angles. Some cautiously and circumspectly, carefully searching for landmines and hidden bogeys; some with carefree abandon, enthusiastically jumping at the first glittering objective that catches their eye; some with resignation, accepting whatever life throws at them; others with dogged loyalty and blinkered determination following life's dutiful path; and many other variants according to how our individual entwined umbilical and life-created Gordian cords incline or compel us. All approaches hold their own truth as well as their limitations, so it might be wise to discern through as many lenses as possible. Six decades of life experience have taught me that gut feeling and intuition have usually been more reliable discernment tools than reason and intellect: for me that conduit has always been the one from which the Spirit has emerged. Nonetheless, man does have to live by bread as well as learning to live not by bread alone.[22] I needed to take a *pragmatic* leap in faith.

For probably as long as a decade, below the dominant chords of my day-to-day living – professional demands, care of family and friends – there had been a gentle crescendo of background music coming from those canny instruments of my inner life: increasingly gut and heart communicated with head their passionate desire to do something about caring for the carers. I had already spent a three-month period of sabbatical leave – half in UK and half USA – with the focus Needs of the Carers. Through the results of that research and my lifetime involvement I had collected enough evidence to know that there was sufficient unmet need within the church and voluntary sector to justify some additional initiative to what little already existed. So I set about pushing doors to see what resources I could muster to make this my next phase of ministry. I talked to potential funders and followed trails to buildings and other resources which might become available. A group of Roman Catholic nuns in East Anglia was vacating their extensive premises and keen to see them used for the purposes I was proposing, but eventually their French motherhouse decided to sell the assets for commercial gain. A long-established non-denominational Christian community in Sussex were retiring, but chose another proposal with substantial Roman Catholic backing. An established ecumenical venture, on the surface outward-looking and inclusive, expressed interest in absorbing my proposal but on further examination proved below the surface to be restrictive and denominationally exclusive. The last door I knocked was the one I have already described where the new bishop firmly closed the door.

Not for the first time in my life, the New Testament assurances given by Saint Paul were under the microscope: "God is faithful, and he will not let you be tested beyond your strength, but with the testing he will also provide the way out so that you may be able to endure it."[23] Because my senior clerical friend was so keen that I take the vacant appointment at the retreat centre, I had held on for interviews to take place until less than a month before (at my own choosing) my eighteen-year long appointment would end and with it my family accommodation have to be vacated. Time was now of the essence. As my employers were giving me the equivalent to six months' salary, I decided to treat this as a period of sabbatical leave where I could consider potential paths forward at my leisure. I contemplated perhaps a leisurely long voyage on a cargo ship, along with other fanciful ways I could unwind from the demands of eighteen years' labours. Until, on a Sunday evening, with my belongings packed into boxes on top of which my two cats sat, they seemed to ask inquisitively: "And US?" Oh dear. I had forgotten about these faithful companions of the last couple of years. Sharing the dilemma with one of my daughters, within a few hours through a contact of hers I was offered the use of a delightful tiny cottage located on Bredon Hill near Tewkesbury. *Noah's Ark* was its name and Noah's Ark became its purpose for me: a perfect retreat to hide away in, pray, ponder and prepare.

During my last few weeks at Mansfield colleagues and friends expressed their gratitude generously. My official farewell celebration was combined with the inauguration of the two merged charities, Aston-Mansfield – appropriately marking the end of one era and the beginning of another for them and for me. Of the many kind gifts I received, the least in monetary value, and the one I treasure most, came from the staff of one small project – a leather pen and pencil case with an inscribed brass plaque: *"Thanks for Caring* From Your Friends at Mansfield". It is kept in the same faith-strengthening memory box as the Jerusalem Bible I inherited and the oak roll-top desk I was given. The Board of Trustees dined me out separately at one of their Pall Mall gentlemen's clubs, inviting me to bring my two daughters as partners. Alone in the gentlemen's loo the Settlement's President (former Chairman of crashing tray fame, who once explained that he was probably too heterosexual to understand what it meant to be homosexual) turned and said: "I did enjoy having your two tempting daughters each side of me tonight." May my spirit allow me to say something similar – but slightly different – when I am ninety-one, I thought!

So that chapter was over. Setting out for Noah's Ark on Bredon Hill, car laden with the little I would need for six months' recuperation, I murmured to my complaining cats: I wonder if Abraham had his cats with him in 2000 BCE when he set out for Ur after God had told him to leave his country, his family and his father's house for the land He would show him?

On our first morning together in the Ark, I chanced upon this pearl of Goethe's wisdom:

On burning boats

Until you leave behind a chapter of your life, with no way of return, you are still hesitating, you can still draw back; consequently, your energy will be scattered, not focused.

When you do let go, 'Providence' also moves, moves

towards you with gifts. 'Events' begin to happen.

Encounters surprise you with what you need.

Material assistance comes to you unexpectedly.

None of these things could you have 'dreamed up'.

You can never be aware of what is waiting for you at the right moment.[24]

Chapter Seven

Discernment

Years Sixty-two to Seventy-five
What does it really mean to grow old? For me... to be old is to be myself. No matter how patriarchy may classify and categorize me as invisible and powerless, I exist. I am an ongoing person, a sexual being, a person who struggles, for whom there are important issues to explore, new things to learn, challenges to meet, beginnings to make, risks to take, endings to ponder. Even though some of my options are diminished, there are new paths ahead.
Shevy Healey

Waiting for me on that first sunny January Monday morning in 2001 was a blank piece of paper. I began to write on it with relish then drove from my fittingly named Noah's Ark the half-hour journey to Great Malvern and wandered aimlessly around the shops with no other purpose than to buy provisions for the week and a couple of wineglasses – there being none in the cottage! Over a leisurely morning coffee I reflected that by this time I would be deep into a pile of post, budget juggling, telephone calls and staff meetings; the inexhaustible pending tray of the normal working round. The only demands ahead of this day were a gentle walk on Bredon Hill and two cats needing me to open a tin of Whiskas. My relief was palpable as an eighteen-year-heavy rucksack was lifting from my shoulders. No one else would make demands on me today. Not a soul had any idea where I was in this coffee shop. Time was my own. I was in heaven.

Only a few weeks of this indolent bliss passed before strips of red and white tape across the Bredon Hill footpaths barred my entry – Foot and Mouth Disease: the ghastly epidemic which lasted from February to October, devastating farm stock and confining the nation's walkers to tarmac roads and lanes. Now looking back, I see the tape as being symbolic of what was unfolding on the wider canvas of my life. Goethe's promise that 'when you leave behind a chapter of your life with no way of return Providence moves towards you with gifts' was not as it appeared to be unfolding for me. After the four false trails during the previous year, three months into my carefree vacuum saw no 'events happening' or 'encounters surprising me': still no answers to the what, where, how, with whom, and who is going to pay me questions. Many might say I should have been hounded with sleepless nights by the uncertainty of my situation. But I was not. The conviction which had come through drums and dance on a Greek island eighteen months before joined the damp wallpaper, Jerusalem Bible and roll-top desk to hold me within the promise: "You can trust God not to let you be tried beyond your strength."[25]

During my last year at Mansfield I had invited five good friends to act as a support group to help me pick my way forward to the unknown future. I had also just circulated details of my hopes and plans for a new project to a wider circle of friends inviting any helpful suggestions. From within a combination of these two initiatives a friend let me know about former colleagues of hers who had left their professional lives in London, pooled their assets and established a unique resource in North Wales for people who wanted to make serious personal explorations or reflections. Perhaps my vision could be incorporated into theirs, she wondered? I followed the trail reluctantly, for North Wales had long been off my personal radar. It was a corner of the UK where I had enjoyed happy holidays but somewhere I felt I could never work or live: weather, language, culture and remoteness from the world I knew in the South of England had flagged up amber and red warning lights. But as this suggestion had reached me on one of my ominous – or propitious – annual Maundy Thursdays I knew I had no option but to push at the door which was now ajar.

I spent a couple of happy days appreciating the substantial contribution these people were making and enjoying their idyllic location near Caernarfon. I was not sure whether it was the right place for me, although at that point I could not put my finger on why I was coming to this decision. Deep within the Snowdon mountain range, as I was returning to Worcestershire, I experienced a rare moment. It was the nearest I have encountered to what is recorded in the Old Testament as *The Calling of Samuel*.[26] It was as though the towering mountains above themselves were shouting at me: "You do not belong here with us but you do belong in this land – Go West!" The experience was quite overwhelming and haunted me for twenty-four hours. The following morning I attended the local Quaker Meeting, returned to the Ark for lunch and put into my computer's search engine the place which I knew from previous holiday visits was west of Snowdonia – the Lleyn Peninsula. Within seconds *"Finding Your Way*, Quiet Day at St Hywen's Church Aberdaron 10am to 4pm – bring your own lunch" scheduled for the next day flashed on my screen. Without hesitation I topped-up the cats' dishes, apologised to them and retraced my steps to that remote corner of north-west Wales. After breakfast at an Aberdaron hotel I walked the dozen steps to the church and was welcomed warmly by bemused participants when they heard my story about driving 180 miles at a moment's notice to join them. Over our sandwich lunch another participant casually mentioned that he had been in Cardiff the previous weekend for a conference. "What a coincidence," I said. "I was booked into a conference in Cardiff last weekend but had to cry-off because of a cold." Our fleeting exchange of glances gave the game away: it was the annual conference of the Lesbian and Gay Christian Movement.

By the end of the day this newfound friend had offered me the use of his house nearby for any visits I needed to make to explore the local area. Later that week one of the Directors at the centre I had visited offered four months' free use of a small local cottage she owned whilst I began my search for suitable property. Goethe was right: Providence *was* providing gifts; events *were* happening; encounters *were* surprising me. Another set of dominoes was beginning to drop into place, but at God's choosing and timing, not mine: indeed, against my personal inclination to go to this forsaken geographical location and later than my impatient soul desired.

This latest cluster of providential indicators, although only circumstantial and which would probably have been written off as coincidental by most people, were sufficient for me to feel confident that the trail was heading in the right direction. But there was an additional compelling factor emerging – something I had never previously been sensitive to: I felt as though the very soil beneath my feet was drawing me to this area. I was becoming convinced this was where I had to be. Within the space of a month I looked at over fifty properties in a confined area of twenty miles by six. Then early one Friday morning I passed a For Sale sign on a remote lane in the middle of the Peninsula, but was unable to trace details in any agent's brochure so backed the car to get sight of the house name. A little old lady appeared, asked if she could help and then invited me in for coffee with her husband. I stayed for a couple of hours; at their invitation revisited the following day; returned on the Sunday without them knowing to walk the local lanes and climb the mountain behind the house; and then at nine o'clock on the Monday morning walked into the estate agent's office to offer the asking price. "Oh yes, Mrs Spencer has just phoned and said she would like you to have the house. I'm glad you've offered the full price for when the locals know it's on the market they'll gobble it up. You can't buy that sort of view every day." There began a lovely friendship with the family. Sadly, I had to take the funeral of the wife in 2004, but that of the husband, aged ninety, not until 2014.

Along the way I was able to offer support to their lesbian daughter who, it transpired, had struggled with her Jehovah Witness mother's entrenched position over the gay issue most of her life. This final piece of evidence dissipated any thoughts I may have had about 'coincidences'. Geoffrey was destined to be a resident of Cymru in the County of Gwynedd.

I was confident I was in the right place to start what I felt called to do for this phase of my vocation: offer support to weary and worn-out caregiving leaders from the Church and wider voluntary sector. But within the context of a life of faith I still had important truths about myself to discover: the grain of wheat again had to fall to the ground and wither before it could bring forth fruit worthy of the table to which I was now being called.[27] Repeated cycles during my adult life had brought me temporarily to a deeper, humbler level of discipleship – failure at King's, dismissal from the RAF, broken marriage, dashed life-partner hopes – but, like a perennial weed, my ego had drawn me back to the more comfortable stratum of worldly achievements.

Against my strong defence of pride, the first lesson to learn was that it was my own batteries which were empty. My unconscious motive for making these life changes was to deal with my own needs: it was *me* who had run out of steam. Up until then I could only acknowledge this reality by projecting on to others that which I was unable to accept about myself: come to me all you others and I will heal you! For someone whose pride was so carefully hidden, someone who felt his shoulders wide enough to bear everyone else's burdens, this was a humbling reality to accept. Indeed, it would take me a number of years on the Lleyn Peninsula, with my life developing in very different ways to how I thought it would, to fully acknowledge this as part of the genetic code of my *true*-self.

Although I had taken the step in faith and moved away from the security of Mansfield, I was still driven largely by my own vision and ambition. My heartfelt prayer had remained 'thy will not mine' but with more than a little hope that thine might be mine! The second lesson I needed to learn was more subtle. Carefully hidden from the outer world, my ego was secretly hoping to see my career going on to even greater heights in worldly achievement by initiating and heading-up a substantial project for my next good cause: the world's well-trodden successful career pattern – private to field marshal, intern to prime minister, curate to bishop. During 2000 my aspirations for a new project were high, but my approaches to large country estates and major grant-making trusts had found none of those doors opening. Even now my vision saw the potential of a small acorn growing into a large oak. A private letter sent to a friend of mine contained a message which I needed to heed: "Do not aim for success or status. Aim to be where you can live as a sign of salvation for the rejected. Do not become unavailable to them by becoming acceptable to those who do not like their comfort disturbed."[28] I knew that my move from the comfortable Cotswolds to East London, on the surface, gave the impression I had moved in the direction of this authentic truth, but my under-lying pride still needed work done on it: I had not yet overcome the temptation of hubris. My spiritual journey was only in its infancy; my inflated ego camouflaged in humble and worthy clothing was not enough. John Lee, an Anglican priest/psychotherapist friend who travelled alongside me when I was first accepting my gay sexuality, suggests that our defences, our roles, our possessions, our status, are all facades, at worst totally obscuring our true self, at best caretakers for that soul-deep self, vulnerable, frightened, yearning.[29]

Of course, these deeper understandings came neither instantly nor painlessly; they emerged over three or four years as my new life unfolded. Ty'n Twll (appropriately translated as 'the little house in the hollow') was a delightful eighteenth century single-storey farm cottage, set within an acre of grounds, south facing with views over sea and mountain. Before the building could be occupied it needed major renovation, particularly to deal with damp. Even then it was too small to undertake the purpose for which I intended it, but had potential for some modest expansion. Money was a major problem. My personal resources only enabled me to purchase forty per cent of the equity and there was no surplus for any building extension or project work. My initial intention was to establish a registered charity, promote my small support group into trustees and get on with what had become my bread and butter for eighteen years – raise grants in order to acquire additional buildings and provide revenue funding. I set out enthusiastically to establish *Via*, the chosen name for the project. I remember my first meeting of the potential trustees where they shared my vision and made suggestions. Afterwards I reflected that it was the little savings that I had which were supporting the project; it was my property and time; and I probably had more experience in this field than any of them – yet they were giving me their instructions. At the same time I discovered that the Charity Commission would not allow a house I owned to be used for charitable purposes, and the Church of England Pension Board – which provided the mortgage for the house – would not allow the property to be used for commercial purposes. On pragmatic grounds alone, I would not be able to continue with the project in its present grandiose form. More significantly, within my deeper self small seeds of authentic spirituality were beginning to bud: words like *humble, little, simple, invisible* began to occupy the foreground and replace their forbearers – *ambitious, enterprising, impressive* and *significant.*

I wrote to the five good friends sacking them from the trusteeship they never began and closed the file on any aspiring new application to the Charity Commission. To the world I was trying to leave behind – my own upwardly thrusting ego and the achieving image and target conscious cultures within society – it might have been seen as failure. There was no epoch-making new venture emerging to restore the flagging spirits of worthy do-gooders, only Bob the Builder with hardly two pennies to rub together, occasionally wondering what insanity had brought him to this predicament. But at the level where truths are known intuitively and instinctively and eclipse rational arguments, there was a deeper peace. I still knew this was the place where I had to be – geographically, economically and spiritually. Only here would Goethe's wisdom have a chance to return.

Unexpectedly and unsolicited, first a friend offered me a loan for a modest extension which could provide independent accommodation for one or two people visiting, and then another friend donated the lump sum from an endowment policy she was due, an amount which covered my basic living expenses for a whole year whilst I was undertaking the cosmetic additions to the extension myself after local builders completed their construction work. A chance meeting at Bangor University encouraged me to update the counselling training I had undertaken during the late 1970s. A postgraduate diploma turned into an MA enabled me to join *Relate* counsellors and a further postgraduate diploma gave me the formal Accreditation with the British Association for Counselling and Psychotherapy that enabled me to start part-time work as a counsellor at local GP surgeries. These therapeutic involvements were neither planned nor anticipated: they simply emerged, ensuring I undertook deeper self-reflection by beaming lasers on to my theology and personal motivation. They also equipped me with better skills and insights as I accompanied others on their journeys, and gave me the means by which I could keep solvent for the next decade by augmenting my pension. Through word of mouth 'punters', as my visitors became affectionately known, trickled in. Mostly, they spent no more than five or six days walking the lanes and coastal paths, enjoying the garden and sharing their personal and professional stories. Somewhere along the way healing balm seemed to seep in.

It had never in my wildest imaginings been my intention or

desire to move to North Wales to live an obscure solitary life. Often I asked myself if I was rationalizing foolishly-made decisions; projecting on to an illusory God the results of my errors of judgement and weak self-preservation instinct? Was I being too simplistic and naive by telling myself that the new life as it was developing was an indicator of divine will; adjusting divine will to suit my changed circumstances? After trying to penetrate as honestly as I could deeper cellars where any unconscious motivation might hide and asking others whose wisdom I respected, I could only conclude that Ty'n Twll, for better for worse, for richer for poorer, seemed to be it – whatever 'it' was. Woody Allen is credited with the adage, "If you want to make God laugh tell him your plans"; an Anglican nun offered an alternative interpretation:

> If we are trying to hand over the control of ourselves to God in order to be used by him in his infinitely vast purposes of reconciliation, we can know that although our trust in him will be tested to the uttermost, it will never be betrayed. He meets us at the point of our deepest desire – often beyond our own articulation – brings us to a pitch of sensitivity where we are conscious of the fears, uncertainties, and anxieties which have to be kept just below the surface in most people's ways of life, and asks us to affirm his love through it all.
> *Mother Jane, SLG*[30]

Like its internal spiritual core, the external manifestation of my faith has been evolving over many years. From the simple belief systems fed by my maternal grandmother and Sunday school teachers, to the meatier diet of theological education put into practice as parish priest and RAF chaplain, I have been questioning and gradually jettisoning doctrines and practices which I find erroneous or no longer helpful. I appreciate the benefits I have derived in the past and accept that for other people these may still be helpful, but my own understanding and needs are continually changing. My developing responses to the doctrines and practices of my faith are not an indictment of others but an attempt to become congruent with my personal spirituality. A mixture of logical reasoning, life events and becoming attuned to my intuition has brought me to my changed conclusions; the insight I have gained through a wide variety of therapeutic modalities has helped me understand much of the provenance of my changing beliefs and the psychological growth paths which have made some aspects redundant.

As I reflect on my life experience I realise how strongly I have been influenced by the 'oughts, shoulds and musts' from catechism, scout laws and parenting. I begin to wonder how many others within the churches are entrapped in what person-centred psychology calls *Conditions of Worth*,[31] where they feel only valued (or value other people) as long as they behave in certain ways or believe certain things. I wonder how many, like me in the past, have repressed their true feelings and displaced them on to less threatening religious practices? When I observe some of the irrational beliefs and practices within the institutional churches it is not difficult to understand how Freud's reasoning brought him to the conclusion that God is a projection brought on by a desire to revert to the state of infantile dependency. The deep and secure faith, which runs through me like the writing through a stick of rock, allows me to examine carefully what I really believe without fear, that I might mistakenly join Freud and throw the baby out with the bath water. I stand wholly alongside the common focus found in many faith traditions believing in the Oneness of a Love-purposed Sustaining Divine Spirit and that the life and teachings of Jesus, and inspired sources from many other faith traditions, show us how we can obtain unity with the One God.

In her introduction to *God in All Worlds*[32] Lucinda Vardey suggests that:

Religion has provided a tenet for spiritual expression and many have turned to it for guidance. The organised religions offer not only a sense of community bound by common beliefs, the collective study of scripture, the performance of ritual and the use of disciplines and practices, commandments and sacraments but also ways of taking care of our souls. Yet spirituality can embrace a wide range of thoughts and experiences – from the mystical to the metaphysical, including psychic episodes and miraculous occurrences in the supernatural realms – and so following an orthodox and traditional religion can sometimes prove limiting.

I have found it beneficial to explore outside the confines of the church into which I was ordained. The Quaker Society of Friends, of which I have been a formal Attender since I have been in Wales, has drawn me by their simplicity and inclusivity. Their sacrificial acts of love shine out: true fruits of the spirit – even if seldom labelled as such. I have been fed by authentic spirituality found in the deeper seams of all the main Christian denominations and within other faiths – particularly the wisdom of Ibn 'Arabi contained within Sufism. Old favourites like Küng, Merton, Nouwen, and the poetry of Rumi and RS Thomas have inspired my meditations; contributions from people like Holloway, Spong, Crossan, Ó Murchú, MacCulloch, Felten and Procter-Murphy have challenged my thinking. I have felt far from alone in any heterodoxy and more than at home within the company of radical believers.

Jim Cotter (Anglican priest and faithful friend for over thirty years) describes *"bad* religion as offering safety and security in the form of a certainty that is the opposite of faith, a control that is the opposite of freedom."[33] A Unitarian Minister, Ralph Helverson, offers an antithesis in words of a hymn, *Impassioned Clay:*[34]

Deep in ourselves resides the religious impulse:
Out of the passions of our clay it rises.

We have religion when we stop deluding ourselves that we are self-sufficient, self-sustaining, or self-derived.

We have religion when we hold some hope beyond the present, some self-respect beyond our failures.

We have religion when our hearts are capable of leaping up at beauty, when our nerves are edged by some dream in the heart.

We have religion when we have an abiding gratitude for all that we have received.

We have religion when we look upon people with all their failings and still find in them good; when we look beyond people to the grandeur in nature and to the purpose in our own heart.

We have religion when we have done all we can, and then in confidence entrust ourselves to the life that is larger than ourselves.

Whilst I was reconfiguring my faith and spirituality during this Welsh period of my life, how was my libido developing? It was difficult to avoid this question in the company of fellow therapists: little passes their beady eyes or twitching noses. I have been blessed during my involvement with *Relate* by being part of a cohort which has become known as my 'harem': three women who, after going through training with me, meet regularly to reflect on therapeutic practice. They have become good friends. Over a meal at my home, knowing I had not been in a relationship for many years and because of past hurts was cautious about forming a new one, they expressed their concern about my solitude and isolation. Cutting to the chase one of them asked: "How many people pass your door each day and of those how many are suitable and available gay men?" "Walking – three to four; eligible – minus one," was my laconic reply.

I acknowledged earlier in the book that after my divorce I

hoped to form a committed relationship and anticipated that I would. Although I have never been proactive in searching for a partner by advertising or using social media, I have always had my antennae attuned. Has it been through the ravages of fate or my own mismanagement that I have ended up as a celibate gay man – or has it been God's will? Whilst being held by the concerned arms of my harem, or close family and other friends on different occasions, I have explored this predicament. I have tried to ask honestly: was it fear; lack of self-confidence; inertia? These and other possibilities have all been examined under psychological and theological microscopes. I suspect the wisdom expressed some years ago by one dear friend, sadly now dead, betrayed the most accurate reason for my long singleness: "You've never really been able to say a Nunc Dimittis (Lord, now lettest thou thy servant depart in peace) to that deep love have you?" He was right. For many years – decades – I have been unable to close (or distinguish even) the gap between fantasy and reality. However much my rational mind has reinforced the stark reality that we have grown in different directions to a point where compatible coupledom is no longer a viable proposition, my heart has countered with those sweet (and very real) memories of yore. I continue to ask: Has our relationship not changed into a close and valued friendship built on nearly four decades of shared history – and now has become nothing more? Is it not time I accept this reality and resolve to move on? Or is mutual love of the sort we found simply *indistinguishable* if two people continue to feel the same about each other? Was that insightful Lebanese poet, Khalil Gibran, right when he asserted: If you love somebody, let them go, for if they return, they were always yours. And if they don't, they never were?

By that time in Wales my libido, no doubt, will have lost some of the persistent dominance it had in its early and middle years, but I think also I had reframed the context of my life: priorities had become reshuffled and energies redirected or *sublimated* – an understanding I have already mentioned is shared by both theological and psychological disciplines. Although I have never displayed a *No Vacancies* sign, I can honestly say I am now content in my singleness even though I still hope it might be otherwise.

I suspect that for a period of at least four of my ten Lleyn years much of my personal libido became sublimated into the Dissertation. Aware that I would like eventually to produce something for publication, I chose *Therapy's Light on the Church's Understanding of Varying Sexualities* as the subject of my MA, which my supervisor invited me to advance into a thesis for a doctorate. Flattered, I continued for a year or two, totally engaged and fulfilled until I ran out of money. But my decision to withdraw was more complex, for a grant or loan could have overcome that hurdle. I questioned my deeper motives for not continuing. At my age the additional qualification would not advance any career and my earlier academic glitches had already been compensated by gaining the two advanced postgraduate diplomas at distinction level. I had nothing more to prove. More importantly, I was able to accept that on the trajectory of my spiritual development my ego needed no extra accolade: humility and simplicity would not be advanced by a doctorate; a Masters would more than suffice.

For four years I researched my topic avidly. I explained in the Introduction to the Dissertation how the Christian Church was at war over its understanding of human sexuality and that I proposed to test the hypothesis that insights from therapeutic disciplines could help the churches accord equal status to sexual minorities. One of the respondents to the dissertation, a therapist who has now left the Roman Catholic Church, summarized the Church's current position with some measure of pessimism:

C of E Reports and Commissions have been produced in abundance, but they have been 'blocked' (repressed out of conscious awareness for they are too frightening) and shelved; the institution collaborates in order to forget. Some would say that it is more than a matter of understanding organisational processes; it is to do with fundamental beliefs. The institution is led by leaders who will use whatever doctrines they can find to support their individual beliefs. Perhaps they are caught up in their own unconscious – for some conscious – processes. The church needs something quite different: champions as leaders who are able to work and speak out with integrity – open and transparent. I wonder if the advances in the secular movement might not encourage (force) the Church to face some of its 'shadows' – those unconscious organisational and individual processes? Society's new attitude might be more effective in bringing about change, offer more influence on self-awareness. The Church might become aware that it is being marginalized by society over issues of sexuality. Sadly those who reach the purple are those who've stayed in the institution and been more servile to their predecessors – a choice that has been colluded with by the laity, who want them there and keep them there.

His opinion was shared by a senior Church of England clergyman who is still working within the establishment:

To be honest, at present I am not optimistic that the churches can institutionally come to a greater understanding over issues around sexual identity. We have painted ourselves into a corner, and perhaps we will shortly have to choose between the growing insights of secular Western society and an increasingly narrow-minded, sectarian understanding of religious faith. I am not at all optimistic.

For me the subject matter of the dissertation was far more than an academic study, it coursed through my veins daily and had become part of my DNA: it was the story of my life and I knew the answers through personal bruises and broken bones. It was not difficult to evidence that varying sexualities are no modern phenomenon, and have been part of human experience from the beginning of recorded history. I tried to do justice to the breadth and depth of the struggle gay men and lesbians have had, and demonstrate how political actions during the last half-century have brought about the changes which had enabled Andrew Sullivan to make such a strident proclamation as this in 1995:

> Before, the homosexual entered public debate and said: "Let us into your military, and protect us from hostility. Let us into your businesses, so we can earn our living without discrimination. Let us into your schools, so that we can affirm our selfworth without fear of rebuke or contempt. Protect us from the harsh words of those who spurn or dislike us, so we can live a more fulfilling and enriching life; free us from the oppression of the traditional family, so that we can live out our lives in protected isolation." Now, the homosexual enters public life and declares: "We are your military and have fought your wars and protected your homes. We are your businessmen (and women), who built and sustained this economy for homosexual and heterosexual alike. We are your teachers; we have built your universities and trained your scholars. We are your civic leaders, your priests, rabbis, your writers and inventors, your sports idols and entrepreneurs. We need nothing from you, but we have much to give back to you. Protect us from nothing, but treat us as you would treat any heterosexual."[35]

My own life experience has brought me to this position too. I reflected in the Dissertation, "I believe his (Sullivan) is a rhetoric that is complementary to the deeper psychological changes that are needed for homosexual equality. It encourages individuals to see themselves as integrated human beings – to view their varying sexualities not as some aberrant private behaviour but as a constitutive part of their identity, in the way that heterosexuality is a constituent part of others' identities; to be proud of their human skills while not denying their gay, lesbian and bisexual natures." Because my personal fate has brought me via a heterosexual route (albeit by experience rather than orientation) I feel acutely the difference between *'belonging by birthright to the fully human race'* (which I experienced when married) and *'being accepted and welcomed into an existing club and given slightly less than full membership'* (the fruits from gay emancipation). Are these not the essential differences between 'Marriage' and 'Civil Partnership'?

What moved me most during the research – and I think became the strongest contribution within the Dissertation – were those personal accounts of the thirty individual respondents (including one archbishop, four bishops, thirteen clergy of both sexes, a nun, two professors, two teachers, and six other lay people) drawn from across different denominations and faiths. At the more conservative end of the different observations, the respondents confirmed that *'Confused.com'* might be an appropriate maxim for all of us to use who have travelled along the Faithful and Gay road – at least for part of our journey. The majority, however, offered far more astringent and penetrating condemnations recording how they, or their clients, had been treated by the churches – as this small sample of their submissions demonstrates:

The institutional church doesn't know what to do with us. This leads to a strange kind of schizophrenia where private and public attitudes are split in a way that leaves us essentially isolated and disempowered. My personal experience has been of many individual expressions of affirmation but each disclosure has had to be carefully chosen... I have never found myself in a position where I have felt able to come out indiscriminately to a whole parish and I have always thought that the very people who have been personally supportive, especially those in the hierarchy, would be far less supportive in that sort of situation. There is still this need for invisibility in many situations and all sorts of variants on the 'don't ask, don't tell' approach... Affirmation is often coupled with either silence or a kind of intellectual fumbling with the issue on the public stage.

C of E Rural Dean and psychotherapist

Two particular incidents have influenced my thinking about the *private* and *public* divide: A Diocesan Bishop took the trouble to write and thank me for my work in sustaining an eighteen-month interregnum. He was certainly aware of my sexuality, because we talked about it. One week later he wrote in the national press that he would never ordain a practising homosexual, nor did he think it compatible with ordained ministry. I find such inconsistencies depressing and undermine commitment. Also unless (Archbishop) Rowan has changed his views substantially since he was chaplain of Westcott House (Theological College) when I was a student there, I find his contortionist attempts to maintain unity at all costs dispiriting, to say the least. Of course, I understand that he doesn't want things to fall apart on his watch, but in the end the cause of truth is ill-served by expediently clinging to a bogus unity. I am tempted to focus on the *real* world of the parish and ignore hierarchies as nothing but a pack of cards.

C of E Rural Dean

The weight and force of defence mechanisms – projection, repression, denial, regression, displacement, rationalization – can be as relentless and devastating in their effect as giant waves of a tsunami against primitive sea defences. What other explanation could cause people to hold so strongly to literalistic interpretations of the bible in the face of contemporary biblical understanding? What other explanation could allow people, whose personal spirituality values *integrity* so highly, adopt a dominant discourse when they are addressing the issue of sexual equality that places *unity of organisational structures* above what they have previously identified as the *truth*?

What bishops do with their 'internal selves' is amazing; are they not aware of the unconscious processes that force them to still hold on to the Don't ask, Don't tell policy? What unconscious processes of fear and guilt are at work below the surface to fly in the face of contemporary evidence (about sexuality); what self-deception is seeping into their unconscious actions in order to sustain self-preservation at the expense of integrity? The 'internal' and 'external' divide is amazing.

RC Priest and psychotherapist

I have known scores of fellow pilgrims – people of faith who are trying to be true to their same-sexual orientation – extremely well over the years, either through friendship or professional involvement. Whilst accepting that everyone retains his or her individual cultural and psychological uniqueness, I have come to identify a number of different groupings, or clusters, of similarly-inclined and like-responding travellers. Some have their tentacles in more than one of the groupings or may move during a lifetime from one to another, progressing or regressing in obedience to the tugs from internal or external influences; others remain encased in one or more of the same groupings, held in the grip of their unconscious compulsion or consciously making a personal choice to stay there.

In the latter category I have known many who are content and happy to stay within the safety of a more rigid belief structure knowing that their sexual orientation, if it is expressed and known about, would place them outside their religious bodies. A twenty-two year old student saw me for his allotted ten NHS sessions with a focus on his depression. Classically, ten minutes before the end of the final session, having insisted for the previous three or four how much better he was feeling, he suddenly exclaimed: "I don't know; I'm feeling so depressed now that it's even made me think I might be bisexual." From his assessment session forward I had intuited (accurately as it now transpired) what his underlying dilemma might have been, but he had fended-off all my attempts to encourage deeper investigation. Now, having established a trusting therapeutic relationship with me, in desperation and at the very last minute, he lowered his defences. An extended two or three sessions at least allowed me to make him aware of other Christian options to the one his fundamentalist sect was insisting on. Although he soon advanced his self-identification from bisexual to gay, he remained firmly committed to his cultural background and to his year's full-time voluntary commitment to a church sect, who permitted no sex of any sort outside of heterosexual marriage and did everything to convince him that his self-identification as gay was incorrect – 'everything will be fine when you meet the right girl'. He was a lovely, good, kind and sensitive young man; I feel confident that he will always remember our last three sessions, whatever happens to him. He now knows he has Christian options. There have been many other pastoral cases and friends in similar situations.

From my theological college days onwards I have known a number of gay priests who have had difficulty in integrating faith and sexuality. The ones I have known have usually come from the catholic end of the churchmanship spectrum, where some therapists would see use of The Confessional encouraging the *splitting* process. A therapist respondent for my dissertation who had recently been received into the Roman Catholic Church remarked:

> The Church is very capable of making a psychological split
> allowing pastoral life and moral/ethical life to exist side by
> side with contradictory expressions of sexuality: the confes-
> sional is a helpful enabling tool which can allow one belief to
> be outwardly and officially expressed whilst condoning
> another practice. There are lots of dark corners with cobwebs
> growing over them: bishops and parish priests can have
> private views, and private lifestyles, but there is pressure – of
> which they may or may not be conscious – to toe the line
> publicly.

I have been a member of this cluster myself in the past and
attribute my journey out of it partly to observing bachelor friends
(free of responsibilities of marriage and children) who have
stayed closeted within a Jekyll and Hyde pattern of living. Some
– sadly a number who have died prematurely – have used alcohol
and extravagant living as a coping mechanism; others have been
tempted by the prospect of promotion – the lure of red piping on
black cassocks or exchange for the purple. Now from the fringe
of the institutional church, I am sad to see this phenomenon
continues into the twenty-first century, despite the avalanche of
new medical, psychological and theological understanding about
homosexuality. I was grateful to a close friend of some ten years
when he observed: "I have always thought you were just boringly
obsessed with the gay issue: I now see it was your father's abhorrence of cant and hypocrisy that has encouraged you to be
concerned about many aspects of integrity."

Integrity inevitably finds its different expression according to
a person's individual circumstances; as I reflected about my deep
love relationship, we each underwent our own painful journey in
order to reach "our *different* integrities". I can only observe the
lives of other people and make decisions about my own. I cannot

judge or condemn others. And I would want to be the first to acknowledge that many gay people of faith, ordained and lay, have made a fully conscious choice about their faith adherence and their lifestyle, and chosen to remain celibate. But when one thing is said or preached and another enacted, then my blood pressure rises.

The *Don't ask, don't tell* – or only partly ask, partly tell – cluster can be comprised both of people of faith and people of non-faith. Some seem to be governed, or half-governed, by the requirements of their religious adherence; others either by societal expectations and norms or their own psychological restrictions. Conservatism and pragmatism are invariably common drivers. They appear able to conform, or half-conform, to religious or societal requirements and at the same time express their own – or accept others' – sexuality privately, or semi-privately.

Because of my personal history it is not surprising that a number of friends and clients have shared with me their dilemmas as married people. No matter how close you are to anyone as friend or therapist, you can only glimpse a small fraction of the whole picture from outside anyone's intimate relationship. I can never say more than "I think I know something of your pain" or "can imagine the difficulty you are facing in making a decision". Various permutations have been shared over the years: married and splitting-up or staying together; with or without children; when the children are infants, adolescents or adults; when the couple say it has been a mutually agreed decision, or a one-sided one; when separate lives are lived secretly, or when everyone tells all; when only half- or three-quarters of the truth is shared; when nothing is said but everything is known. Many have been able to say they were as homosexual or lesbian as you can be by orientation but for reasons of platonic love and loyalty to their spouse (their marriage vows), love and duty towards children, career demands, finances, wider systemic circumstances – often a mixture of all – they maintain their heterosexual facade and lifestyle alongside a secret gay fantasy life and, for some, activity. Whilst critics might accuse them of having the best of both worlds by enjoying their cake and eating it, in my experience most have been floundering in the turbulent waters between *integrity* and *pragmatism*. Every situation I have known has had a different outcome: confusion, stress and pain seem to be the only common denominators.

The gay continuum is well documented in professional studies to indicate that there are considerable variations. The majority of statistics evidence that most people know themselves whether their sexual orientation is gay or lesbian, with a minority being in a grey band, including some who would point to having a 'genuine' or 'total' bisexuality which they say makes them feel as though they are incomplete unless they follow both avenues. Many people in this grouping have shared their stories. For some it can be a very confusing place to be. All authorities acknowledge that external circumstances can influence an individual temporarily – during our experimental adolescent years, in same-sex situations when deprived of opposite-sex companionship, and so on. For many (like the young client I mentioned earlier) I have found the label 'bisexual' can be a gentle stepping stone on the way to owning the fully gay label, especially when having to talk about these matters in public. Many will remember the furore that followed when an Anglican Archbishop honestly acknowledged his sexuality was "in a *grey area* but that [he] had always endeavoured to lead a celibate life." I remember a Roman Catholic priest colleague who chose an alternative phrase: "I have a *floating* sexuality."

Then there is the cluster of those who are principally attracted to people of their own sex at an emotional and erotic level who have passed through one or more of the other groupings and have now integrated their faith and varying sexuality. They have emerged from the fog of *'Confused.com'* to *'I-know-who-I-am-and-what-I-believe(or not).com.'*: the coming home that Andrew Sullivan described as being like a black and white movie that suddenly converted to colour. Many have shed their tears of joy (and fear) with me during a counselling session and received a congratulatory good wish hug appropriately at the end; many times has a celebratory drink – or two – been enjoyed in a pub or living room with friends.

Sadly, from my perspective, a number of friends and clients have lost their faith in the process of gaining clarity over their sexual orientation – identifying themselves as gay, bisexual or, in a few cases, straight when they had previously thought they were gay. The two – faith and sexuality – are not necessarily interconnected of course; there are as many routes to clarity about faith or non-faith as there are to awareness of sexuality. And I have been as humbled by the generosity of my atheist friends as I have been disappointed by the egotism of some people of faith.

To have had the privilege of friends and clients sharing with me at these depths has been one of life's greatest gifts. Words used frequently by gay people – *confused, hurt, rejected, ashamed, guilt-ridden, isolated, disempowered, patronised* – are gradually being replaced by those more frequently used in the past by heterosexuals – *overjoyed, normal, accepted, affirmed, supported.* Increasingly, to borrow imagery from another therapist, "Those who have been turned into frogs by their experience of the world – their family and cultural scripting – are turning back into princes and princesses."[36]

During my years on the Lleyn both my daughters started families of their own and, in turn, moved to the same village in Mid Wales fifty miles away from me. Visiting them one weekend I surprised myself by announcing over breakfast that I thought I should move to the same area: what did they think? Within twelve months Goethe's familiar sequence was repeated: providence provided; events happened; unexpected encounters surprised me. I moved into a house four hundred yards away from one family and six hundred from the other. The decision had been taken with the same intuitive conviction that thirty years before had found me unexpectedly moving from the Cotswolds to East London and two decades later to the wilds of North Wales, but this time without needing prompting by any wallpaper, bible, desk or African drums: I just *knew* this was where I had to be.

Now, having settled here for three years, I return to the Lleyn to visit friends and look upon it as a far and distant land, but with treasured memories and gratitude for the unexpected gifts it brought: lasting friendships; solitude and peace; time to think; and a new vision. It had given birth to no aspirational projects; no acorns grown into oaks; only invisible shuffles in the direction of simplicity and trust – which perhaps was the acorn which was meant to have grown into an oak! It helped me identify with the reflection offered by Henri Nouwen during the most difficult period of his life:

As you come to realise that God is beckoning you to a greater hiddenness, do not be afraid of that invitation. Over the years you have allowed the voices that call you to action and great visibility to dominate your life. You still think, even against your best intuitions, that you need to do things and be seen in order to follow your vocation. But you are now discovering what God's voice is saying, "Stay home, and trust that your life will be fruitful even when hidden."

It is not going to be easy to listen to God's call. Your insecurity, your self-doubt, and your great need for affirmation make you lose trust in your inner voice and run away from yourself. But you know that God speaks to you through your inner voice and that you will find joy and peace only if you follow it.[37]

Here, in my new wet and wooded – but sunny – valley I am quickly discovering a community of mask-free pilgrims who, in wonderfully varied ways, trek along that same path of shared values and simple trust.

A friend has recently described this evening period of life as a time when you and your teeth sleep in different rooms, when you need two shoves up to get out of an armchair, and when you increasingly find yourself talking about the good old days. I know what he means. Recently, my two year old grandson thought it hilariously funny to make a grab in the swimming baths at my small plate of four front teeth; I was only too pleased to tell his six year old sister more stories of times when grandad was a naughty boy and to tell her nine year old cousin stories of when grandad too was obsessed with pen knives and mountain survival shelters. At this stage of life teeth are invariably an embarrassment; reminiscing, never a chore.

I know that autobiographical reflections come more from historical sunspots than shadows; nonetheless, composing these chapters has been good for my soul. Jung has said, "One does not become enlightened by imagining figures of light, but by making the darkness conscious."[38] Seeing my seventy-five years in one chunk has been humbling, and acknowledging the constant trail of signposts and links that have brought me through the darkness as well as the light has super-charged my faith. It has been – is being – a life of amazing blessings. Prophesy from Isaiah has come true: *"Listen to me... (you) whom I have created from the womb / whom I have supported since you were conceived. / Until your old age I shall be the same, / until your hair is grey I shall carry you. / As I have done, so I shall support you..."*[39] In life's autumn days, more than any before perhaps, I can echo the words of Augustine: "Thou hast made me for Thyself and my heart is restless until it rests in Thee." I understand now why Michael Ramsay was able to say: "As I get older, I believe more and more about less and less."[40]

Eberhard Bethge speaks of Dietrich Bonhoeffer "undergo(ing) the agony of universal rejection... physical and psychological isolation... without any attempt at justification...":[41] the hard and harsh invitation that lies near the centre of most world religions. The Christian brand, into which I was baptised in those fragile emergency days and ordained into two and a half decades later, knows well the painful and slow process of being stripped of all delusions and preconceived ideas about ourselves in order that we can grow to our full glory. We all have to find – or are given – our unique path for this journey. Often I feel the *Via Crucis* others find themselves travelling makes my modest gay struggle pale into insignificance: terminal illnesses, bereavements, famines, natural disasters, broken relationships, wars, redundancies, extreme poverty – so many agonizing paths.

What is amazing is how many times the routes the divine indicators have taken me on have become paths of redemption. Other than my relationship with my children, which will always come first, nowhere does the redemption seem greater than when the damp wallpaper led me to East and West Ham. There, the shattered pieces of Mansfield's historical scandal were able to be put back together and produce a vessel of new glory. From it being a frighteningly homophobic institution, I witnessed changes which enabled many of us to live openly in gay partnerships; the institution give birth to the first Christian HIV/AIDS support project in East London; and a full equal opportunities policy to be implemented where it was a disciplinary offence for anyone – including trustees – to discriminate on grounds of sexual diversity.

James Alison, Roman Catholic priest and theologian, has captured my life's experience of faith and sexuality in one succinct paragraph:

What is becoming apparent is that there is a more or less

regular minority of people of both sexes who, entirely independent of circumstance, war, long journeys, imprisonment, cults and so on, simply are principally attracted to people of their own sex at an emotional and erotic level. It is furthermore becoming clear that this is in most cases a stable and lifelong feature of who these people are, is not in any sense a dysfunction and does not in any way diminish the viability of the people who just are this way. And it is even beginning to become clear that such people are able to develop and receive that full-heartedness of love for each other, that delicate birth of a being-taken out of themselves for the other which is not just lust, nor a defect of some other sort of love which they really ought to have, but don't seem to be able to, but is quite simply the real thing, which, when present, is recognised as a gift from, and an access to God.[42]

I experienced this reality intensely during my profound love relationship when words attributed to St Paul resonated loudly: "everything that is true, everything that is noble, everything that is good and pure"; "the three things that last: faith, hope and love; and the greatest of these is love."[43]

In 1979 I joined the group of counsellors for the Gay Christian Movement (now LGCM), coordinated by Jim Cotter. He was a young Anglican Priest 'destined for higher things' until the mid-1970s, when he was Chaplain of a Cambridge College, he dared to acknowledge his sexuality publicly, became a co-founder of the Gay Christian Movement and started writing about how a Christian could be faithful and gay. For many hundreds of us he was a rare beacon of light and hope. There followed a 'ministry outside the gate' for twenty-two years as a freelance author, spiritual director, liturgist and faithful evangelist until his last three working years as vicar of Aberdaron – where I had attended the quiet day eight years before. Our lives interwove closely as friends over thirty-five years, particularly when he went through the shadows of mental health and physical illnesses. In 2014 I was privileged to be alongside him during the last three days of his debilitating leukaemia, when from Monday to Wednesday in Holy Week he gradually faded away. On his last morning I cradled his body on the floor after he had fallen out of bed, waiting for three-quarters of an hour until an ambulance crew arrived to help him back into bed. Frail and gaunt, with emaciated limbs, I saw a symbol of what many in the Church had done to him over the years for declaring the sanctity of same-sex love. The words of the wise Mother Jane shared in *Loving God Whatever*, the book Jim had compiled, came to mind: "Are we willing to feel skinned, afraid and isolated, and to say a Gethsemane Yes with Jesus to life – and death – as they come to us? Therein is the reality of obedience."[44]

Then, sitting for his remaining hours quietly at his bedside, I picked up a book he had been reading. Michael Mayne, the former Dean of Westminster Abbey, had written:

Oscar Wilde, being transferred from Pentonville to Reading Gaol on a rainy November afternoon in 1895, stands handcuffed and in prison clothing for half an hour on the platform at Clapham Junction where a crowd begins to form, first laughing and then jeering him. It must have seemed an eternity. One man recognised him and spits in his face. "For a year after that was done to me," wrote Wilde, "I wept every day at the same hour and for the same space of time."[45]

Jim died peacefully with my hands in blessing on his head late on Wednesday afternoon. After keeping vigil alone with him in his flat that night, I escorted the undertakers the following morning to the hearse and remembered it was *Maundy Thursday* – again! My mobile phone rang and my 'profound love' drew my attention to a sonnet by Malcolm Guite which had just been shared on the web for the Wednesday in Holy Week:

The Anointing at Bethany

Come close with Mary, Martha, Lazarus,
So close the candles stir with their soft breath,
And kindle heart and soul to flame within us,
Lit by these mysteries of life and death.
For beauty now begins the final movement,
In quietness and intimate encounter,
The alabaster jar of precious ointment
Is broken open for the world's true lover.

The whole room richly fills to feast the senses
With all the yearning such a fragrance brings,
The heart is mourning but the spirit dances,
Here at the very centre of all things,
Here at the meeting place of love and loss
We all foresee, and see beyond the cross.[46]

References

1. Freud, S. (1907) *Obsessive Actions and Religious Practices*, Hogarth, London
2. Mayne, M. (2006) *The Enduring Melody*, DLT, London
3. Avis, M. and Cotter, J., eds. (2006) *Loving God Whatever*, Cairns, Harlech
4. https://sites.google.com/site/peternobletalks/faith-religion-1
5. Vardey, L. (1995) *God in All Worlds*, Pantheon Books, New York
6. Sullivan, A. (1995) *Virtually Normal*, Picador, London
7. O'Brien, K. *www.theguardian.com/news* (4 April 2014)
8. Haggard, T. *www.christianitytoday.com* (22 November 2013)
9. Yeats, WB (1972) *The Circus Animals' Desertation*, OUP, Oxford
10. Eliot, TS (1943) *Burnt Norton (Four Quartets)*, Harcourt, NY
11. Titus Lucretius, first century BCE Roman poet and philosopher
12. Herbert, G. (1995) *The Complete English Works*, Everyman's Library
13. Rahner, K. (1960) *Encounters with Silence*, St Augustine's Press, UK
14. Hebrews 12:1 – Jerusalem Bible version
15. Thomas, RS (2000) *Collected Poems*, Phoenix, London
16. Shakespeare's *Othello* – Desdemona choosing between husband and father
17. Expression often used to refer to Jesus Christ
18. Mayne, M. (1998) *Pray, Love, Remember*, DLT, London
19. Sullivan, A. (1995) *Virtually Normal*, Picador, London
20. British Association of Settlements and Social Action Centres
21. International Federation of Settlements
22. Matthew 4:4ff, *Man does not live by bread alone*
23. 1 Corinthians 10:13 – New Revised Standard Version

24. Adapted by Cotter, J. (2001) *Waymarks* (10 August), Cairns, Sheffield

25. 1 Corinthians 10:13 – Jerusalem Bible version

26. Reference to 1 Samuel 3:4ff

27. John 12:24, *Unless a grain of wheat falls to the ground...*

28. Avis, M. and Cotter, J., eds. (2006) *Loving God Whatever*, Cairns, Harlech

29. Lee, J. quoted in Cotter, J. (2001) *Waymarks* (11 November), Cairns, Sheffield

30. Avis, M. and Cotter, J., eds. (2006) *Loving God Whatever*, Cairns, Harlech

31. Rogers, CR (1951) *Client-Centred Therapy*, Constable, London

32. Vardey, L. (1995) *God in All Worlds*, Pantheon, New York

33. Cotter, J. (2001) *Waymarks* (16 March), Cairns, Sheffield

34. Helverson, RN (1993) *Singing the Living Tradition*, MA: Boston UUA

35. Sullivan, A. (1995) *Virtually Normal*, Picador, London

36. Perlman, G., Davies and Neal, eds. (2000) *Pink Therapy Two*, OUP, Bucks

37. Nouwen, H. (1997) *The Inner Voice of Love*, DLT, London

38. Jung, C. (1983) *Vol. 13 – Alchemical Studies*, Princeton UP, US

39. Isaiah 46:3–4 in Jerusalem Bible version

40. https://sites.google.com/site/peternobletalks/faith-religion-1

41. Bethge, E. (2000) *Bonhoeffer: Theologian Christian*, Fortress Press, USA

42. Alison, J. (2010) *Broken Hearts and New Creations*, DLT, London

43. Philippians 4:8 and 1 Corinthians 13:13, Jerusalem Bible version

44. Avis, M. and Cotter, J., eds. (2006) *Loving God Whatever*, Cairns, Harlech

45. Mayne, M. (1998) *Pray, Love, Remember*, DLT, London

46. http://malcolmguite.wordpress.com/2012/04/04/the-anointing-at-bethany/

CHRISTIAN
ALTERNATIVE

Throughout the two thousand years of Christian tradition there have been, and still are, groups and individuals that exist in the margins and upon the edge of faith. But in Christianity's contrapuntal history it has often been these outcasts and pioneers that have forged contemporary orthodoxy out of former radicalism as belief evolves to engage with and encompass the ever-changing social and scientific realities. Real faith lies not in the comfortable certainties of the Orthodox, but somewhere in a half-glimpsed hinterland on the dirt track to Emmaus, where the Death of God meets the Resurrection, where the supernatural Christ meets the historical Jesus, and where the revolution liberates both the oppressed and the oppressors.

Welcome to Christian Alternative... a space at the edge where the light shines through.